VICTORIAN
CANVASWORK

VICTORIAN
CANVASWORK

Kathryn Brennand

David & Charles

To my mother and father for all their support; to Peter and my children, Laura, Nicole and Matthew, for all their understanding.

Created and produced by Rosemary Wilkinson
4 Lonsdale Square, London N1 1EN

Art editor: Frances de Rees
Illustrators: Sheilagh Noble, Mary Tomlin
Photographer: Tracey Orme

Typeset by Fakenham Photosetting Ltd
and printed in Singapore by C S Graphics Pte Ltd
for David & Charles plc
Brunel House   Newton Abbot   Devon

British Library Cataloguing-in-Publication Data
Brennand, Kathryn
    Victorian Canvaswork
    I. Title
    746.44
ISBN 0–7153–9944–6

CONTENTS

Introduction

The charts from which the projects in this book are worked are reproductions of original charts from Berlin in Germany and Vienna in Austria, produced in the mid-nineteenth century. They would originally have been stitched using wools dyed in Berlin, thus the embroidery produced from them was called 'Berlin woolwork'. This became so popular in the Victorian era that it became practically synonymous with Victorian canvaswork.

The very first chart is said to have been produced in Germany around 1805, but mass production did not get underway until the 1830s. One of the most prolific publishers of the charts was a German called L. W. Wittich, whose artistic wife is said to have recognised the potential of these charts for the wealthy women of the period. For the first time they would have a fully-coloured pattern, in which each square represented one stitch, so that the designs could be reproduced exactly. Most of Herr Wittich's designs were of a very good quality, with clear colour painting and very attractive patterns. He continued to publish Berlin patterns for well over thirty years, during which time he manufactured and produced in excess of 1,400 patterns.

One of his patterns is reproduced in this book and has been stitched for the Flower Cushion (page 41). There are also charts from other Berlin publishers: A. Todt, Hertz & Wegener and M. Levy, and a good selection from two Viennese publishers: H. F. Müller and Franz Barth. Unfortunately, however, little is known of these firms.

The charts were produced by a two-part process. The background grid was printed, then the designs were hand-painted by women, who did the work to earn a little extra money. Some of the grids were made up of tiny squares, which must have been very difficult to paint with individual colours. The chart for the Teacosy on pages 120–1, for example, has 24 squares to the inch. The women apparently used square-ended brushes to speed up the process. In several of the charts black symbols have been used inside the squares to mark out the outline of a shape or to distinguish different shades within a shape, but this does not appear to be done consistently throughout a chart: see the Flower Cushion chart (page 41), for example. For the Lily chart on page 46 the painter has roughly sketched in the contours of the leaves before painting in the squares.

From Germany and England the popularity of Berlin woolwork spread throughout the western world. In the latter half of the nineteenth century it

JOURNAL DES DAMES & DES DEMOISELLES.
(ÉDITION BELGE)

Mars 1856

SAJOU 52 Rue de Rambuteau à Paris.

This chart was printed in colour and published by a French women's magazine, also distributed in Belgium. In England the 'Englishwoman's Domestic Magazine' and 'The Young Englishwoman's Magazine' similarly printed patterns on a regular basis.

could be found in, for example, France, Austria, America, Australia and New Zealand, and the production of the charts was no longer confined to the publishers in Berlin or in England.

BERLIN DESIGNS

Predominantly, the pictorial scenes used throughout the whole of Berlin woolwork would be representations of a family pet, pets of the royalty, hunting scenes, shooting scenes and, the most popular of all, posies and garlands of flowers. During the Victorian period flowers were given their own little language, so that you could send a 'message' to a lover or a fond relation by the type of flowers you sent them. Further information on this language of flowers is given with various of the charts within the book.

Many of the flowers portrayed in the charts are perfect illustrations of recognisable species and it is a pleasure to rediscover them. The lilies in the Footstool, the Canterbury bells in the Bellpull and the hollyhocks in the Picture are good examples. The use of four or five shades of one colour in each flower gives them a very natural look, but it is not just the careful selection of colours which makes them so lifelike – it is also the size of the canvas on which they are worked. The finer the canvas, the more like a painting the design appears.

Exotic birds and brightly-coloured insects and beasts of all kinds were also portrayed in the designs. Parrots were particularly popular in England and America and remained in favour for many years; there are two particularly fine examples of parrot designs in this book.

Themes produced in Berlin woolwork were not simply worked as pictures to be framed, but were adapted into patterns to decorate nearly every possible household item, with examples of bellpulls, carpets, tablemats, chair seats, footstools, firescreens and cushions, the latter being the most popular of all, as they decorated people's rooms and were used for comfort on the settees. The Victorian needlewomen also made items of clothing, especially for men, such as waistcoats, smoking caps, braces and slippers.

B E A D W O R K

Some of the beading was worked in what came to be known as grisaille *motifs. These were worked in black, grey and white beads against a strong single-colour background, as in the angel motif above.*

Towards the 1850s a large amount of beadwork was being introduced into the Berlin wool patterns. The beads were mostly used on designs for footstools and teapot stands, slippers, bags, purses and curtain tiebacks. Precious bags were the most popular item to be stitched in beadwork, and even today you can see these exquisite bags in many antique shops or private collections. The patterns for working with beads rather than wool would appear to be for a smaller scale than those for wool, though there were three sizes of beads available and most charts could be adapted.

T H E   B E R L I N   W O O L W O R K   T R A D I T I O N

True Berlin woolwork was almost completely confined to the nineteenth century. There were critics at the time who were noted for saying that the design and production of these charts were very crude and brash, and that the colours they used were too bright and devoid of any taste. This was undoubtedly true of some of the charts, but there was also a wealth of amazing work. It probably reached its peak of popularity during the 1850s and '60s; thereafter there was a slight levelling off, followed by a gradual decline. However, Berlin woolwork continued to be worked until around 1930.

From 1860 towards the end of the century various people, particularly

William Morris, a British craftsman-designer, and his associates, contributed to a movement which endeavoured to bring about a revival of a good and highly classical decorative art within Britain. The ideas of this group were to affect considerably the type of embroidery produced in the late nineteenth and early twentieth century. This was the *art nouveau* period, and its emphasis on natural qualities ultimately led to an upsurge of renewed interest in art needlework.

The aim of this book is to combine the two traditions. It provides a selection of Berlin charts reworked to the same colours as the originals and made into a wide variety of decorative pieces for the home. With each chart there is also a section of suggestions for free adaptations, giving adventurous needleworkers the chance to experiment with stitches, threads and patterns.

The charts are all from the Rachel Kay-Shuttleworth Collection at Gawthorpe Hall in Lancashire. The Hon Rachel Kay-Shuttleworth (1886–1967) spent her whole life collecting embroideries from all over the world and gathered together some wonderful pieces. There are some 14,000 items in the Collection, including Chinese emperors' robes, Queen Anne quilting, embroidered bedspreads and a particularly fine collection of lace. There are also many fine examples of the original hand-painted Berlin patterns, which are beautiful objects in their own right. The following projects present a selection of the best.

During the peak of activity, chart designers reproduced many designs from well-known artists, as well as illustrations from popular novels. Landseer's animal studies were a favourite subject – the photograph shows a particularly fine example of one such interpretation.

Materials and techniques

CANVAS

Canvaswork, or needlepoint as it is also called, is carried out on a special open weave fabric made of cotton or linen and available in different sizes. The sizes are usually measured by the number of holes there are per inch (HPI). They are sometimes also measured by the number of mesh to the inch, a mesh being the intersection of each vertical and horizontal thread. Mesh is also the general term given to the grade of the canvas, from a very fine mesh, known as *petit point*, which can be as small as 30 holes to each inch (2.5cm), to a larger mesh, *gros point*, with as few as five holes to the inch. *Petit point* canvas usually refers to one with 16 or more holes to the inch; a *gros point* canvas has fewer than 16 holes. The greater the number of holes per inch, the smaller the stitches. This usually means that the design on the chart being followed will be reduced and the embroidery will have a better durability.

When deciding on the correct mesh to use, it is necessary to look at any fine detail in the chosen design, the thickness of thread and the required size of the finished product. If the design is to be a bold one without a great amount of detail, then 10 to 14 holes to the inch would be suitable, but for a fairly fine, intricate design 16 to 20 holes to the inch would be more appropriate. For cushions, chair seats, pictures and wall hangings I find 10 to 16 HPI very good. For smaller, finer articles like bags, spectacle cases, pincushions and box panels a mesh of 18 holes upwards is better. Stool tops and rugs work well with an 8 HPI canvas.

The size of a finished piece of canvaswork depends mainly on the size of the canvas used. This can be calculated by counting the number of squares on the chart and dividing it by the mesh size of the canvas. At the back of the book you will find a handy chart giving a series of dimensions for each project for different mesh sizes from 8 to 20 mesh, so that if you prefer to use a different canvas from the one specified in the project instructions you have an automatic guide to how this will change the dimensions of the finished embroidery.

Once the dimensions of an embroidery are calculated, then the correct size canvas can be bought, allowing an extra 2 to 3in(5 to 8cm) all round for ease of working.

Canvas is available in several different types. Those used most often are single thread (or mono), interlock and double (often known as Penelope). It also comes in a variety of widths from 24 to 40in(60 to 100cm).

Single or mono canvas

Single (mono) canvas has single vertical and horizontal threads woven alternately under and over each other. It is available in a large range of colours and sizes. The most readily available is white, followed by natural brown, unbleached, known as antique, and an off white or ecru. (See also Colouring the canvas background, on page 27.)

Interlock canvas

On an interlock canvas, each vertical thread is actually two thinner threads that have been twisted around each other and a single horizontal thread to produce a 'locked' single mesh. Interlock canvas is more stable than the mesh of a single canvas. It is available in white or ecru and is a very good canvas for beginners to use.

Double or Penelope canvas

The third canvas type is a double-threaded fabric. Here the interwoven threads are grouped in pairs. Besides being strong, a double mesh has a further advantage: by treating the double threads as singles, smaller, finer stitches can be made in selected areas where finer detail is required so that, for example, a 10 HPI double mesh canvas becomes a 20 HPI single. This is known as 'pricking the ground' and was a technique often used for facial features in Victorian canvaswork pictures. Double canvas is available in white and antique.

For the best results when buying canvas for the needlepoint in this book, buy the type of canvas that is suggested. However, if it is difficult to get hold of the correct mesh size or type of canvas, then you can buy one that is very similar. If there are one or two stitches more or fewer, this will not make a great deal of difference to the style of the needlepoint. You must be very careful that you also buy the correct amount of yarn. If you are using a larger mesh canvas then you require more yarn.

JOINING CANVASES

It is better to avoid having a seam in a piece of canvas embroidery, as the canvas can become very bulky when several layers have to be put together and stitched over. It is essential that the embroidery canvas should be measured to the correct size before starting a project. However, if it is necessary to join two pieces of canvas, before you work any stitches place the two canvases together, overlapping where the seam should be by at least 1in(2.5cm), and tack together. Once the canvases are positioned together accurately, the stitches can be worked over both layers, so hiding any join.

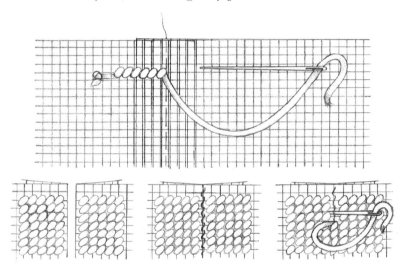

Canvases can also be joined once they have been worked by overlapping or whipping a seam. To do this, fold the canvas back, leaving a single unworked thread on either piece of the canvases to be joined. Oversew together, then work a row of stitches over the top, thus giving a piece of embroidery that does not appear to have any seams within it.

YARNS

The most commonly used threads are of pure wool and are specially manufactured for embroidery. This is because wool is an inherently strong fibre that has proved very durable in canvaswork. There are three types of pure wool suitable for canvaswork. In describing the construction of these threads, the terms 'strand' and 'ply' are used. For example, Paterna Persian yarn is made up of three strands, each of which consists of two plies. Strands can be separated easily, plies are better left as they are.

All of the projects in this book have been worked in Paterna Persian yarn. There is also a conversion table on pages 126 to 127 giving some guidance on the equivalent shade numbers for other wool brands.

Paterna Persian yarn is a three-stranded, two-ply yarn slightly thicker than crewel. All the wool used to make this yarn comes from the first time sheep are shorn when they are about fifteen months old. This gives longer wool than at subsequent shearings, which are at twelve-month intervals. The length of the wool at shearing has an effect on the hairiness of the yarn: 10in(25cm) long wool fibres will have half as many fibre ends and therefore be less hairy than a similar yarn made from 5in(12.5cm) long wool fibres. During the spinning process the yarn is 'polished', which both reduces the hairiness of the yarn and produces a surface finish which gives a light lustre to the final colours.

The three strands are loosely twisted and can be easily separated, giving the needleworker the flexibility of using one, two or three strands to suit the size of canvas or to mix strands of different shades together.

The number of strands used depends on the type of stitch as well as the mesh size of the canvas. In general, one more strand is used for a vertical or horizontal stitch than for a diagonal stitch on the same size canvas.

If you are using more or fewer than three strands, cut the required length of yarn, separate the strands and put together the number required, but do not twist the strands together before threading the needle.

Each project states the number of strands to use, but the table below gives details of the number of strands appropriate to the different mesh sizes, should you wish to change the canvas.

Crewel yarn is a two-ply yarn manufactured with one strand only. It is generally used with a few strands in the needle. It is quite soft and fine and can be blended with more than one colour, as with Persian yarn.

Tapestry yarn is a smooth, four-ply yarn, also manufactured with one strand only. Used in a single strand it is suitable for stitching on medium-sized canvases.

Strands and needle sizes for different canvases			
canvas mesh (single)	*vertical or horizontal stitches*	*diagonal stitches*	*needle size*
10	4 strands	3 strands	18
12	3 strands	2 strands	20
13	3 strands	2 strands	20
14	3 strands	2 strands	20
16	2 strands	1 strand	22
18	2 strands	1 strand	24
20	1 strand	1 strand	24

Other threads

To add further effects to an embroidery a large variety of different threads may be used. Metallic threads are extremely good for highlighting an area, used on their own or mixed in with a few strands of Persian yarn. Silk, coton perlé and rayon all have similar uses for producing variety to a design, as shown in the sample adaptation of the butterfly design on page 85, for example.

QUANTITY

When buying yarns for the canvaswork in this book, you will be able to duplicate the designs exactly by using the brand and shade numbers specified with each project. If you would like to substitute the yarns for another brand, refer to the table at the back of the book or use the design charts to get the correct colour tones. Also, don't think that you have to follow my colours exactly: be brave and make your own colour choice, or even add some extra colours where you think fit.

It is advisable to buy sufficient yarn to complete the project, particularly for the background if you want to have an even colour. Although with modern technology dye lots are very similar, there may still be some slight differences which could cause a visible colour variation within your background. If you find that you need to buy more threads, it is often better to mix some of the new stitches in with the old, thus creating a slightly speckled background.

Where no specific quantity of yarn is given with the project details, you will need one skein or a part of one skein. Where a number of lengths has been specified, this is based on one length measuring 18in(45cm). Many of the leftover shades will be useful for other projects. Note that the quantities given are based on the project being worked in half cross stitch (see page 23) unless otherwise stated. Tent stitch or cross stitch will require more yarn.

NEEDLES

The main needle used in canvaswork is the tapestry needle. This has a large eye that can be threaded easily and a blunt end, so that it does not split the canvas thread. Tapestry needles are available in a range of sizes from 13, the heaviest, to 26, the finest. Select the needle size according to the mesh of the canvas being worked (see the chart opposite and instructions with the individual projects). For a particular piece of work, the most suitable needle will have an eye large enough to allow the chosen yarn to be threaded through easily and to pass smoothly through the holes of the canvas.

MEASUREMENTS

Measurements have been given in imperial and metric throughout the book. Inches have been rounded up to the nearest ¼in and centimetres to the nearest 0.5cm. Follow only one set of measurements for a particular project; do not change halfway through as they are not exact equivalents.

FRAMES

Canvaswork is usually stitched in an embroidery frame, but small articles can be hand held. Personally, I like working small needlepoint projects in the hand because I find them easier to manipulate and perfect for carrying with me wherever I go. However, I prefer to work larger pieces on a frame – but it is important for each embroiderer to do what is most comfortable. It is advisable to take the decision about whether or not to use a frame at the very beginning of any project rather than half way through, as a frame will create a different tension from working in the hand.

The advantage of working on a frame is that it helps keep the canvas taut, making it easier to work. A frame also prevents the canvas from being severely distorted as it is worked. If the canvas is worked in the hand, the stitches, especially tent stitch, tend to pull the work out of shape, with the result that a large piece of embroidery often requires a great amount of reshaping by blocking and stretching on completion.

Most frames for canvaswork are square or rectangular. The popular embroidery frame – the round tambour frame – will distort the fabric and is therefore not recommended. There are several different types of frame available, the easiest and simplest of which is the stretcher frame, which can be made from an old picture frame or from two pairs of artist's stretchers. These are available from all specialist embroidery or artist's suppliers. A homemade frame using four pieces of wood and mitred corners is adequate, so long as the frame does not easily twist out of shape.

For any large piece of embroidery, a commercially made frame is normally far better. The best ones to use are the slate or rotating frames. Some of these are supplied with a stand (below right), thus freeing both hands for the stitching. One hand can be kept above the canvas and the other beneath it, enabling the needle to be passed quickly up and down through the holes in the canvas. Rotating frames (below left) are the ones most readily available and can be used for all basic canvaswork projects.

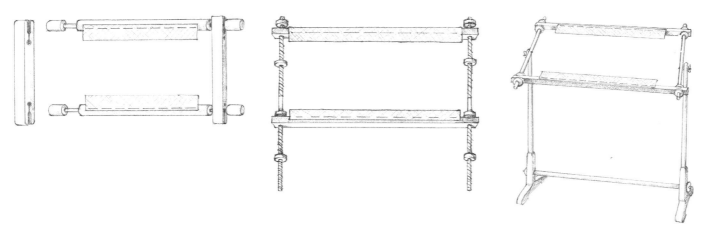

Preparing the fabric

Before placing the canvas on to any frame the edges must be protected from fraying. Masking tape is very useful for this purpose, and should be doubled up over the edges and pressed into position using the blunt end of a spoon. This helps to keep the tape secure for the duration of the embroidery project. If the project is a large one and will be on the frame for several months, then the sides should preferably be protected by stitching tapes over the edges. This also prevents the canvas from fraying when it is pulled tightly onto the stretcher frame. Use a fine, flexible bias tape about 1½in(4cm) wide, double it over the edges of the canvas and attach with straight running stitches.

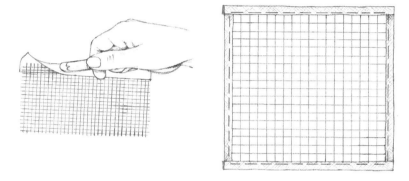

Fitting a canvas to the frame

Whichever frame is chosen, the canvas must be fixed squarely onto it, so that the horizontal and the vertical threads are exactly aligned with the edges.

A stretcher frame should be made to the same size as the piece of unworked canvas. Attach the canvas to the frame using three-pronged silk pins or strong upholstery pins. Alternatively, use a staple gun, placing the staples at an angle to the canvas threads, so that they are not split. To choose a slate or rotating frame for your canvas, consider the following:

- The canvas can be narrower but not wider than the tapes on the frame.
- The canvas should not be shorter than the side bars but it can be longer, since the extra length can be rolled onto the bars at top and bottom.

Before attaching the canvas to the frame, mark the top and bottom of the canvas, so that you may recognise the correct direction of the embroidery should you have to reverse the frame when stitching.

To put the canvas squarely into the frame, first fold it in half, then fold again into quarters. Mark the fold points at the edges of the canvas, either with a pen or a line of tacking. Turn under about five rows of canvas. This gives a strong line of canvas which will not easily fray. Then, taking the top of the canvas, match the centre point of the canvas to the centre point of the webbing on the frame. Using a strong sewing cotton, oversew the edges together. Work outwards from the centre, first to one edge of the canvas, then to the other, fastening off the threads securely at both ends. Attach the bottom edge of the piece of canvas to the other roller in the same manner.

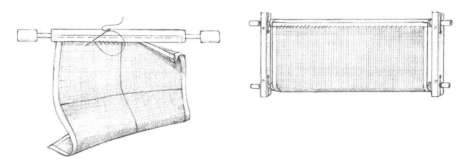

Next, roll the canvas up to the correct size to fit the side bars and put the side bars in position at each end of the rollers. Fix them by means of the screws or wing-nuts. Still using the strong sewing cotton, now lace the sides of the canvas over the sides of the frame. This will keep the fabric evenly tight in all directions. However, if the canvas has been wound round the rollers, the sides will need to be relaced each time the canvas is unwound ready to be stitched.

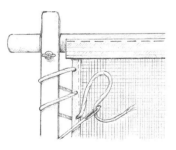

*B*LOCKING AND STRETCHING

To restore the shape of a piece of canvas after stitching, the correct method to use is what is known as 'blocking and stretching', which involves dampening the fabric to enable it to be stretched out onto a soft board and pinned into the original shape. Great care should be taken with canvaswork, as the thread can sometimes be damaged by excessive water.

To make a blocking board, use a piece of soft wood or chipboard and pad it with an old blanket, towel or similar material. Cover the padding with a piece of thin cotton which has been marked out with a square grid using an indelible ink – this helps you to square up the canvas to its original shape. To block the embroidery, spray the canvas lightly with water on both sides to dampen it and place on the blocking board with the right side of the embroidery uppermost. Never flatten a piece of textured embroidery by laying it upside down when blocking.

If complete soaking would not be suitable for a particular piece of work, spraying onto the blanket first and then lightly onto the embroidery may be more advisable. If the embroidery is not suitable for any amount of water, then it should be stretched dry and left for several days until the threads have readjusted to their previous shape, but this method is not quite as successful as the previous one which uses a little water.

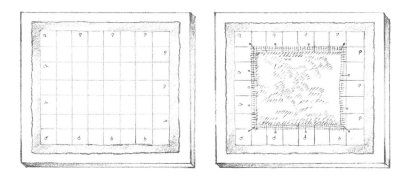

Using rustproof drawing pins, strong upholstery pins or 'T' (macramé) pins, ease the piece of embroidery into shape. To do this, pin the centre top and bottom, centre right and left, then work outwards to the corners, easing the work into the correct shape. Cover loosely with tissue paper to keep the surface clean. All pieces of work should be allowed to dry naturally, away from too much artificial heat.

If the embroidery is still out of shape when removed from the board, repeat the blocking and stretching.

FOLLOWING A CHARTED DESIGN

All the needlepoint designs in this book are worked from charted designs. Transferring the design onto canvas is principally a matter of counting the number of squares of a particular colour, then working this number of stitches in an equivalent position on the canvas.

Remember that each square on the graph paper represents one mesh or one stitch; therefore it should be the thread that is counted when working out the positioning of a stitch.

The charts in this book are exact reproductions of the original, hand-painted charts. For ease of working, it may help to get the charts enlarged on a colour photocopier, or you may find a line magnifier useful. This is in the form of a ruler which magnifies a few rows of a chart at a time. A daylight simulation bulb is a help if you are working in artificial light in the evening, as well as in natural light during the day.

It is useful to make a darker line on the chart for every tenth line of the grid. Some 10 HPI canvas is woven with a darker thread for every tenth horizontal and vertical line, which is very helpful in following the charts. You could mark your own canvas of whatever mesh in the same way, using a fabric pen.

Begin by marking the outside dimensions of the whole design onto the canvas (details are given with each project). Do this either with a watersoluble pen or by a line of tacking stitches. Also mark the centre of the canvas by folding in half, then in quarters.

Where you start to stitch is a personal choice. I have given suggestions with each project depending on the size and complexity of the design. Each row of a plain background colour should be worked in the same direction, ie work from right to left, then at the end of the row, cut off the thread and start again at the right hand side. This gives a more even finish to the stitching. You may, however, stitch from right to left, then at the end of the row turn the canvas upsidedown and continue stitching – this reduces the number of times you need to start and finish the yarn, but creates a slightly ridged appearance.

With most charted designs small blocks of colour are spread out over several rows. When stitching these it is better to start at the top or bottom of the patch and stitch all of that area of colour. A small loop of thread may be passed from one patch to another at the back of the work to a maximum of ½in(1.5cm); this avoids the unnecessary starting and finishing of threads after only a few stitches. If a longer loop is made it will tend to distort the canvas. When working the more complex patterns it is also advisable to have several threaded needles on the go at once: this saves a lot of rethreading when changing colours.

The shade details with each project are grouped by flower, part of design or colour. Within these groups the shades are graded numerically from dark to light, with '1' being the darkest. In some places in these antique charts the colours have faded or the paper has been creased by the original owner. If you are uncertain which of two colours a particular square should be, go for either. The shading in all of the charts is so subtle that your choice will produce the desired effect.

STITCHES

When starting any embroidery project, and particularly if it is on canvas, there are two main points to observe:

- Ensure that the thickness of the thread is compatible with the mesh of the canvas. If the thread is too thick, the stitches will push the canvas to one side; if it is too thin, the canvas will show through the finished work.
- The stitches should be completed to the correct tension throughout the whole work. Stitches that are worked too loosely can cause the threads to stand out from the surface of the canvas, then they are susceptible to snagging when the canvaswork is actually in use. If the tension is too tight it will pull the canvas to one side, and in some cases it may become so distorted that it will be difficult to stitch more than five rows.

There are many canvaswork stitches. The most familiar stitch is a small slanted one, known as 'tent stitch' with its variations 'basketweave tent stitch' and 'continental tent stitch'. It is also the most basic of the stitches and one that all embroiderers should be able to master. Half cross stitch has the same appearance on the surface as tent stitch but is worked slightly differently (see below).

The best way to learn any stitch is to work a sample on the same mesh canvas as will be used for the particular project you have chosen to work.

Work your samples using different thicknesses of thread and different sizes of canvas, so that you can refer back to these at a later date.

When choosing a stitch for a project, consider the amount of wear the finished piece will get. For instance, if you wanted something very hardwearing, then I would recommend tent stitch rather than half cross stitch, however, it does use more thread. Consider, also, the type of canvas being used – half cross stitch can be particularly difficult to work on a single (mono) canvas, as the stitches slip at the mesh points.

In the following details I have chosen stitches that are commonly worked on canvas and would have been used originally in the working of these Berlin charts. I have also shown some of the stitches which are not so familiar but which can be used in your creative adaptations of the charts. Once the patterns have been worked traditionally, you may wish to have fun experimenting with the various stitches. For example, where there are several different flowers in the design, you could stitch one in cross stitch, one in basketweave tent stitch, one in half cross stitch, one with darning stitches and another in beads. This makes an exciting and relatively easy way of adapting the charts to produce your own unique designs.

Tent stitch (continental)

This is worked as a small diagonal stitch over one intersection (mesh) of canvas. It can be worked horizontally or vertically and shows a long stitch on the wrong side. It does not matter which way the stitch slants on the surface as long as it is consistent.

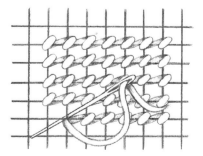 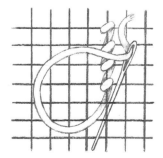

Tent stitch (basketweave)

Basketweave is a version of tent stitch which is worked diagonally. Its main advantages over tent stitch are that it hardly distorts the canvas at all, and that you can work the runs backwards and forwards without having to turn the canvas or fasten off the threads. This of course speeds up the stitching and uses less thread. It is ideal for working the larger areas of background colour. Make sure that the stitches on the surface all slant the same way, unless, of course, you have chosen to reverse alternate rows for a decorative effect.

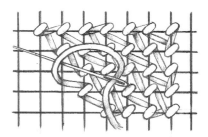

Half cross stitch

This stitch is more economical on yarn, but less firm. The stitch appears the same as tent stitch on the front, but covers only the horizontal thread of the canvas on the back. It is best worked on either interlock or double (Penelope) canvas. If worked on single (mono) canvas the stitches slip under the intersecting threads. This stitch should also always slant in the same direction on the surface. It is preferable to work rows in the same direction, as described on page 20, unless a ridged surface texture is preferred.

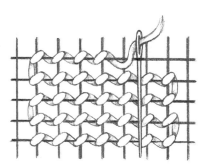

Cross stitch

This stitch is made up of two diagonal stitches which form a cross at the centre. It is usually worked over one mesh of single or double canvas. It can be worked in different ways but the important thing is for the top half of the stitch always to be slanting the same way. Because it uses, in effect, double the amount of wool used for a half cross stitch, it is a good, hardwearing stitch, which does not distort the canvas, but which for the same reason takes longer to complete.

 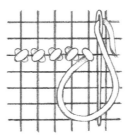

Darning stitch

This type of stitch has several variations. I have recommended a free interpretation of pattern darning in some of the chart adaptations. This is done in rows of straight stitches with varying lengths and widths to create a pattern on the surface of the canvas. It is very similar to using large tacking stitches.

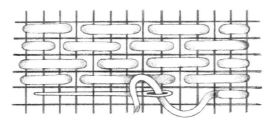

Straight gobelin stitch

This stitch is worked over one vertical and at least two horizontal threads. It may be worked over more threads, so long as the stitches are kept vertical. The canvas may be reversed at the end of a row to give continuous stitching. Depending on the thickness of the thread, the canvas may show through the stitching, so care must be taken to choose the correct number of strands; alternatively the canvas could be dyed to the appropriate colour (see page 27).

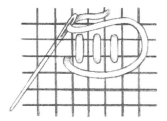 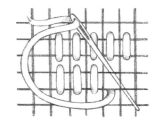

Encroaching gobelin stitch is a variation in which the second row begins on the same horizontal thread as the previous row.

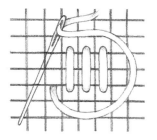 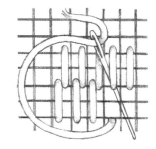

French knots

French knots are used as surface decoration in some of the free-stitched adaptations of the charts. The important points are to use the right thickness of threads so that the completed knot will not slip through the canvas hole, to secure the thread at the back of the work before you start to stitch and to work over one mesh of the canvas.

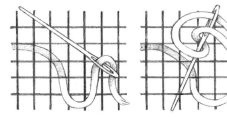 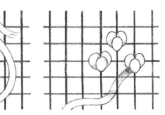

Machine zig-zag

This stitch can be used on some of the chart adaptations if you have a basic knowledge of machine embroidery. Set your machine at the widest zig-zag possible and at satin stitch or 1 or 2 for the length, depending on canvas size. Thread the machine with any combination of colours and cottons or silks as desired, then, following the straight lines of the canvas, machine stitch over the canvas threads. This technique whips the canvas threads with your chosen threads. On a coarse mesh canvas just one thread will be covered – on finer canvases you have a choice.

STARTING AND FINISHING A THREAD

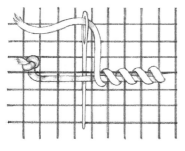

Make a knot at the end of the thread and take the needle down through the canvas to the underside about 1in(2.5cm) away from the point where the stitching is to start, bring it up at this point and pull the thread through, leaving the knot on the surface. As the stitching progresses, the thread underneath will be covered, thus anchoring it down, and when the stitching is completed in this particular area the knot can be snipped away, leaving a nice, tidy surface back and front.

When the length of yarn has been stitched, take the needle through to the underside of the embroidery and thread it through about six of the worked stitches, again anchoring the thread sufficiently well for you to trim off the surplus. This process should be repeated each time a new thread is introduced onto the canvas. This way of working keeps the back of the work neat and free of bulky areas of thread.

We have now covered all the basic techniques that are required before you start your project. We have covered the fabrics, the threads, the frames which enable you to mount the embroidery, the stitches for covering the canvas and their correct tensions.

Now you are ready to start your project pieces and for this there are a few extra tips to make life easier:

- Never use very long lengths of embroidery thread, 8in(20cm) is quite adequate for any project. The longer the thread, the more times it has to pass through the canvas and the more likely it will be to fray.
- Prepare all threads by splitting as required before starting and have sufficient ready to work with.
- Place a knot in the end cut from the skein and thread the needle at the other to lessen the twisting of the yarn.

Additional techniques

COLOURING THE CANVAS BACKGROUND

If the canvas shows through even if you are using the maximum number of strands possible for the mesh and the needle, use an ecru or buff-coloured canvas. Alternatively, try dyeing your canvas with a fabric dye. This has the added advantage that you do not necessarily have to stitch the whole of the background in, thus producing a slightly different effect from traditional needle-point.

Paint the dye onto the canvas, leave to dry, then iron in order to fix the dye and make it colourfast.

ADAPTING THE STITCHED BACKGROUNDS

The simplest adaptation is to change the colour of the background stitching from a plain black to a plain cream, for example. Various alternative background colours are given in the shade details for some of the projects to guide you in this choice. You could also alter the background colour by mixing two or more colours of wool in the needle, so that a shaded effect is produced.

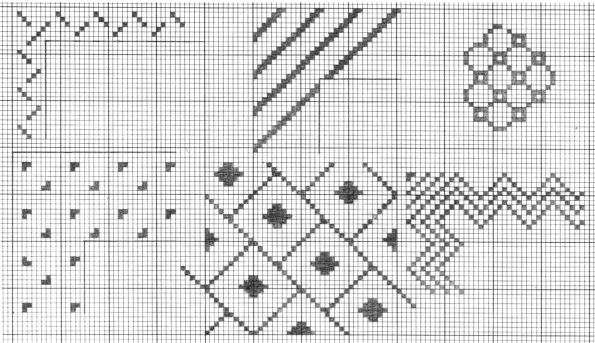

You could decide to increase the background area of the chart, so that the design is set within a much larger 'frame'. This provides the opportunity to create patterns in the stitchery. Lines of equal width could be created diagonally, horizontally or vertically. Alternatively, the stripes thus created could vary in width. You could use just two colours for the stripes, for example cream with pale blue, or you could have a range of colours such as green, blue, cream and black. However, remember at all times that this should be an integral part of the embroidery and not detract from the impact of the central design.

The background pattern could also be made with spots or little dashes in a second colour. You may decide to take this idea further and draft out a more complicated pattern on graph paper. Try some simple geometric shapes, a chequerboard effect, a honeycomb or a chevron pattern (see previous page).

STITCHING BEADS WITHIN CANVASWORK

Beads add a rich, luxurious quality to any design. Rocaille beads are the best type to use, the size depending on the mesh of the canvas. Any item which is to have a combination of stitches and beading should be stitched with threads first. The beads are then stitched on top with a slightly finer thread. A beading needle may be needed if the smallest bead and finest canvas are being used, otherwise select a needle that will fit through the hole in the bead.

Working in tent stitch or half cross stitch, start with the needle on the underside of the embroidery. Hold the bead in place and bring the needle up at the beginning of the stitch, through the bead, and back to the underside at the end of the stitch. Repeat as necessary.

MAKING A CORD

The addition of a cord to cushions, needlecases and spectacles cases provides a highly decorative finishing touch. Cords are extremely easy to produce, especially in their simplest form; however, it is always wise to work a small sample first in order to test the results – cords can use up quite a lot of thread and it would be a shame to waste the threads if the cord produced was too short or too thin for its purpose.

First decide on the style of thread and thickness of cord required: a thin thread will need to be used in multiple lengths to achieve a reasonable thickness of cord. Next, measure the distance around the area which the cord is to decorate. You will need three times this amount of thread used in anything from 2 to 30 lengths, depending on the fineness of the thread. It is essential that you have a minimum of 2 threads.

Put a knot in both ends. Anchor one end of the threads on some kind of hook, which will stay firm while the threads are being twisted. Place a pencil inbetween the threads at the opposite end. Twist the pencil round and round until the threads are tightly twisted together. The longer the cord, of course, the more difficult it is to make and the more twisting it requires. Your initial sample piece of cord should indicate how much you need to twist the threads. If the cord is to have a very tight twist, then twist the threads until they begin to curl up and buckle.

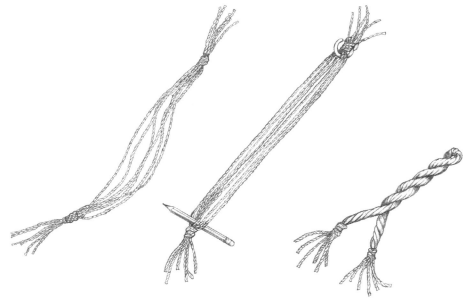

Once the twisting is finished, fold the cord in half, unhook the anchored end, hold both ends taut, then very gently allow the folded end to twist back on itself. The two halves will intertwine, giving a cord that is a third of the original length of the threads. Make a new knot at the knotted end of the cord and trim off the surplus thread.

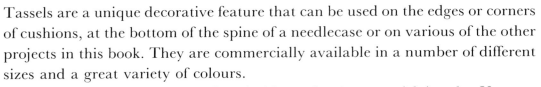

MAKING A TRADITIONAL TASSEL

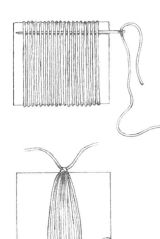

Tassels are a unique decorative feature that can be used on the edges or corners of cushions, at the bottom of the spine of a needlecase or on various of the other projects in this book. They are commercially available in a number of different sizes and a great variety of colours.

To make your own tassel, first decide on the size you wish it to be. You can use very fine or thick threads or a combination of both, but try to balance the length against the thickness. Decide on the length of the tassel and add an extra $\frac{1}{10}$in(2mm): this caters for the natural springiness in the thread once it has been wrapped and trimmed.

Cut a piece of very firm card (such as mountboard) to the length of the tassel and about 2in(5cm) wide. Wrap the chosen thread or threads round and round the card until you feel you have the right thickness of threads, then cut a matching or coordinating piece of thread, long enough to knot round the threads and to sew the finished tassel onto the piece it is to decorate. Thread this piece into a needle and pass the needle underneath the threads on one side of the card, until the thread has been pulled halfway through. Hold both ends of this thread and pull it to the top of the card, then tie the ends together, pulling the threads on the card tightly together.

Using sharp scissors, slide one blade of the scissors underneath the threads at the bottom end of the card and cut the threads along this edge. Take care not to pull the threads out of alignment at this point.

To finish off the tassel, determine the size that the head and neck will be and measure this amount down from the knot. Cut another matching or co-ordinating piece of thread long enough to whip the tassel together to hold the threads firmly in place. Let one end of this thread hang below the tassel, then make a loop at the top. Begin whipping at the point where the neck of the tassel will end. Wrap the thread tightly round the tassel, butting each new loop up to the last until the required depth of neck is achieved.

Thread the end of the whipping thread through the loop created earlier, holding it tightly in place. Take the long thread from below the tassel and pull hard. This pulls the last thread behind the whipping thread of the neck, anchoring it and preventing it from unravelling. Trim any uneven threads.

MIRRORS

Try placing a pocket mirror or a mirror tile upright on any of the designs and see how the combined image and its reflection alters the pattern. Place the mirror across the pattern vertically, horizontally or diagonally until you find the best effect. Mark this with a soft pencil line. Work the design exactly from the chart up to this point, then complete by working the pattern in reverse.

Mirrors can also be used to produce corners in an otherwise straight border pattern. Place the upright mirror at a 45° angle to the design and it will reflect the design at right angles.

A third and most interesting variation is to create a four-way mirror image of a selected area of the design. For this you will need two pocket mirrors or mirror tiles. Tape them together so that they form a 90° angle. Move them across the chart until you find the most satisfying area, then mark this spot with two soft pencil lines. Now make a window template with two pieces of paper cut into 'L' shapes and paperclip these to the page, so that only the chosen section is visible.

To transfer this four-way design to canvas, start stitching at the centre, threading up several colours at once, so that you can progress with different parts of the design at the same time.

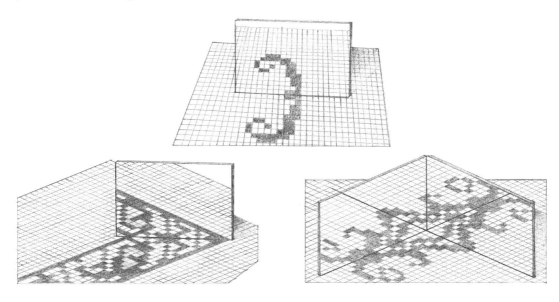

Spectacles case

This project offers two options. The front and back of the case may be stitched in the two different designs, alternatively the same design can be used twice. For the spectacles case in the photograph, both designs were used. The following details therefore refer to the whole chart.

This chart was chosen for its geometric pattern: the four-way repeat on each design gives it a quite different quality from the asymmetrical flower groups.

Dimensions

Larger pattern (excluding background)

45 stitches wide = 3¾in(9.5cm)

81 stitches deep = 6¾in(17.5cm)

Canvas

12 mesh interlock canvas. The front and back are worked as one piece, therefore allow double the larger pattern plus sufficient for the background, as well as an extra 3in(7.5cm) all around the size of the finished embroidery including the background for ease of working. Therefore, canvas size needed:

width: [3¾in(9.5cm) × 2] + 2¾in(7cm) + 6in(15cm) = 16¼in(41cm)

length: 6¾in(17.5cm) + 1½in(4cm) + 6in(15cm) = 14¼in(36.5cm)

Other materials

Tapestry needle size 20

Colour co-ordinated lining fabric

Cord

SHADE DETAILS

2 strands of Paterna Persian
yarn
19 shades used

purples
1 dark D117
2 light D127

greens
1 dark 520
2 light D502

yellows
1 dark 723
2 medium 725
3 light 727

blues
1 dark 501
2 white 260 (1 length)
3 medium 543
4 light 545

oranges
1 charcoal 221
2 dark red 900
3 red 840
4 orange 832 (2 skeins)

greys
1 charcoal 221
2 dark D346
3 light 203 (2 lengths)

Background
Choose between: black 220; royal blue 541; dark teal blue 520; dark
turquoise 590; dark green 680 (as pictured); yellow 773 (6 skeins)

Stitching sequence

Work in tent stitch (see page 22) as this will give extra padding at the back of the canvas to protect the spectacles.

Outline the size of the finished design onto canvas, allowing an extra strip of background five stitches wide in the centre to accommodate the folding of the canvas and two extra rows at top and bottom. There are various options for the shaping of the case. The ends could be curved, following the shape of the patterns, or squared off or a combination of the two. The spectacles case in the photograph was made with square ends. Check the size of your spectacles against the shape on your canvas and allow extra background colour if they are larger than the measurements given. Make sure that the shape and size are very accurate.

Frame the canvas to ensure that there is little distortion, particularly for this project where extreme accuracy is needed. Commence stitching row by row or from the centre point, whichever you prefer. Note that the larger design is not completely symmetrical.

Block and stretch the canvas if necessary.

Making up

As the front and back of the case are worked on one piece of canvas, there is only one side seam. Trim away the unworked canvas to a ½in(1.5cm) seam allowance all round. Cut the lining fabric to the same size and leave to one side until needed.

Turn under the edges of the canvas, so that an unstitched line of canvas is left on all sides. Mitre the corners, as shown on page 64 and herringbone stitch the canvas down.

Fold the case in half lengthwise with wrong sides together. Join the canvas together at the side and bottom of the case by tent stitching through the double

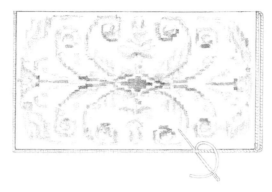

layer of unworked canvas (see diagram).

At the top edge opening, work a row of tent stitch through a single layer of the unstitched canvas and go over the tent stitches a second time at the sides in order to give additional strength at points where the case will receive a lot of wear and tear.

Machine or hand stitch the lining, with right sides together, along the bottom and side edges. Taper the lining inwards towards the bottom edge, this helps it to sit smoothly in the case. Trim away excess seam allowances to reduce the bulkiness. Turn over the top edge of the lining and tack.

Position the lining inside the spectacles case, wrong sides together. Push the lining in place using a square-ended ruler, and slip stitch in place just under the edge into the row of tent stitches. The lining should not show over the top of the case. Remove tacking stitches.

Stitching the cord

The case is decorated with a handmade cord, so that it can be worn round the neck. Measure the distance round your neck to where you would like the case to hang and include the length of both sides of the case. Make a cord to fit following the instructions on page 28. The ends of the cord can simply be knotted leaving the knot on the surface as a decorative feature, as for the case in the photograph. Tie the knot ½in(1.5cm) from the end of the cord and make a self tassel by unravelling the ends. Make sure the knot is securely stitched to prevent it from unravelling.

To stitch the cord in place, knot the sewing thread and insert the needle into the fabric about ½in(1.5cm) away from the beginning of the cord. Bring the needle to the surface beside the cord and pull the thread so that the knot is drawn through the canvas and becomes sandwiched between it and the lining. Using a small stab stitch, stitch into the cord first, then into the very edge of the canvas. Alternatively, a small over stitch placed along the grooves of the cord may be used to couch down the cord. This, however, does not give as strong a finish as the stab stitching.

The case is now ready for use.

Creative adaptations

The colours in the chart could be changed to suit any requirements and the yarn used substituted with different threads, such as a combination of shiny and matt, to add textural interest.

My favourite way of adapting by using mirrors (see page 31) will create many different interesting shapes and patterns, as in the example shown in the photograph.

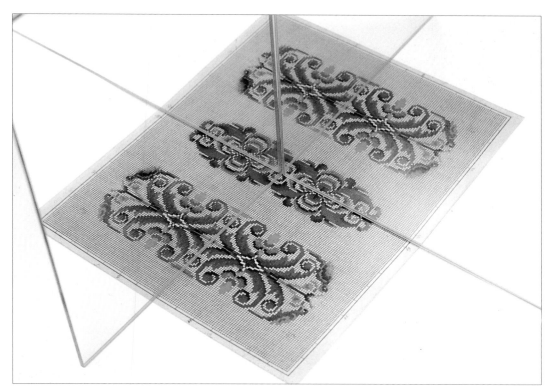

Flower cushion

This cheerful posy of flowers with its subtle balance of colours and flower types is typical of the Berlin patterns. The design has been cleverly constructed so that it can be viewed from any of the four sides and will always look good.

The many shades of green which have been used blend nicely with the delicate tones of white in the rose and yellow in the passion flower. The simple scrolling pattern is used in an effective way at the corners to edge the flowers and bring your attention back to the posy at all times.

During the Victorian era a whole 'language of flowers' was developed, giving each flower a different meaning: thus the yellow passion flower represented religious superstition, the single white rose meant simplicity and *Cobaea scandens* was gossip.

Dimensions
Finished embroidery (including background)
160 stitches wide = 16in(41cm)
160 stitches deep = 16in(41cm)

Canvas
10 mesh interlock canvas. Allow an extra 3in(7.5cm) around the size of the finished embroidery including the background, therefore canvas size needed:
width: 16in(41cm) + 6in(15cm) = 22in(56cm)
length: 16in(41cm) + 6in(15cm) = 22in(56cm)

Other materials
Tapestry needle size 18
Colour co-ordinated backing fabric in wool, cotton, velvet or silk
Cushion pad 16in(41cm) square
Cord if desired
Zip if desired

SHADE DETAILS

3 strands of Paterna Persian
yarn
43 shades used

red flower
1 dark red 840
2 mid red 841
3 dull orange 831
4 orange 832

purple flower
1 dark blue 571
2 dark grey 210
3 dark purple 320
4 mid purple 321
5 light purple 322
6 pale purple 324
7 mid blue 560
8 pale blue 564

centre flower
1 dark grey D346
2 light grey D391
3 dark salmon pink 490
4 mid salmon pink 491
5 very pale pink 493
6 cream 261
7 white 260

pink/grey flower (left)
1 dark pink 911
2 mid pink 913
3 very pale pink 493 (*see* centre flower)
4 light grey D391 (*see* centre flower)

blue-green bud
1 very dark green 660 (2 skeins)
2 dark green 661 (2 skeins)
3 medium green 612
4 light green 663

khaki leaf
1 dark khaki 640
2 mid khaki 641

blue flower
1 very dark blue 570
2 dark blue 500
3 mid blue 341
4 light blue 343
5 bright blue 585

pink flower
1 very dark pink 901
2 dark pink 911 (*see* pink/grey
flower)
3 mid pink 913 (*see* pink/grey
flower)
4 pale pink 491

yellow flower + corner motifs
1 dark yellow 722 (2 skeins)
2 medium yellow 700 (2 skeins)
3 light yellow 711
4 very light yellow 712 (2 skeins)

green leaf
1 very dark green 660 (*see* blue-green bud)
2 dark green 661 (*see* blue-green bud)
3 mid green 601 (2 skeins)
4 moss green 692 (2 skeins)
5 pale green 693 (2 skeins)
6 bright green 671

Background
Choose between: black 220 (as pictured) or charcoal 221 (11 skeins)

Berlin bei L. W. Wittich, Französische Str: No 43.

Stitching sequence and making up

See page 58 for details. The colours of the central flower are faded on the hand-painted chart but they can be worked freely in the white, cream and pinks, so that the colours get darker towards the outside of the petals.

Creative adaptations

Most of the adaptations to the designs in this book have been made either by considering the way we look at the patterns in the chart, or the way we interpret them into hand stitchery. For this design an interesting adaptation would be to combine hand stitchery on a dyed background with a small amount of machine stitching.

For example, to adapt the blue flower, have the machine set to zigzag and stitch a grid in different blues over the intersecting threads (see page 25). Work in this method to cover a considerable amount of the background canvas, then stitch the flower shapes by hand using a variety of threads, to make a nice contrast to the machined work. A sample of this is shown in the photograph.

Lily cushion

The striking balance of colour and shape in this embroidery gives it a unique look compared to the more traditional Berlin patterns. The most appealing aspect is the subtle changes of green against the starkness of the crisp white flowers with their gently bending necks. The design was painted on a lovely bluey-violet paper which blended so well with the flowers that I decided to keep it as the main background colour.
I found a note written on the mounting card to which the chart had been stuck, saying that in the language of flowers lilies of the valley signify the return of happiness. Obviously someone had dearly loved the flowers and had taken great enjoyment in finding their symbolic meaning.

Dimensions
Finished embroidery (including background)
130 stitches wide = 13in(33cm)
130 stitches deep = 13in(33cm)

Canvas
10 mesh interlock canvas. Allow an extra 3in(7.5cm) around the finished embroidery including the background, therefore canvas size needed:
width: 13in(33cm) + 6in(15cm) = 19in(48cm)
length: 13in(33cm) + 6in(15cm) = 19in(48cm)

Other materials
Tapestry needle size 18
Colour co-ordinated backing fabric in wool, cotton, velvet or silk
Cushion pad 13in(33cm) square
Cord
Tassels if desired
Zip if desired

Stitching sequence and making up
See page 58 but note that the whites and creams of this chart have faded with

SHADE DETAILS

3 strands of Paterna Persian
yarn
16 shades used

lilies
1 orange 710
2 yellow 712
3 cream 263 (2 skeins)
4 white 210 (2 skeins)
5 dark blue-green 520
6 sea green D502 (2 skeins)
7 pale green 663 (2 skeins)

blue-green leaves
1 charcoal 221
2 very dark green 660 (2 skeins)
3 dark sea green D500
4 medium sea green D501
5 sea green D502 (*see* lilies)
6 pale green 663 (*see* lilies)

yellow-green leaves
1 very dark green 660 (*see* blue-green leaves)
2 dark green 610
3 green 621
4 pale green 613
5 bright green 694

Background
Choose between: blue-grey 561 (as pictured) or very dark grey-green 530 (11 skeins)

time. Work the flowers with one side white and the other cream – the white always being on the left hand side.

Creative adaptations

Make a window template by cutting two L-shaped pieces of paper and fitting them together to give varying window sizes. Move these about on the chart until you find a pleasing area of colour and pattern. The design will take on an abstract appearance, especially if the window is relatively small.

Temporarily tape the windows to the chart using masking tape or a non-permanent adhesive tape.

Dye the canvas background to blend in with the chosen colour scheme. You may wish to move away from the greens and whites already used. Use a variety of threads and stitches to work the canvas: French knots, tent stitch, cross stitch, or gobelin stitch may be used to add variety, but before stitching consider the final use that this embroidery will be put to. Since this is an adventurous adaptation, traditional methods of stitching may not apply.

8965.

120

Th: Wilh: Meister vorm. A. Todt in Berlin

Tassels are a popular addition to cushions, whether purchased or hand-made (see page 30). They can be used in many different combinations to create different effects. For example, you could stitch a single tassel at each corner or you could stitch three at each corner, combining large and small varieties. The piping cord does not have to follow the outside contours of the cushion – it could slant across the corners to mark off a triangle, which can also be decorated with tassels. The diagrams show some of these ideas, but there are many other combinations for you to explore.

Round cushion

I selected this chart mainly for the enchanting delicacy of the violas. Their vibrant colours, which dominate the design, are often found in gardens today.

The design is broken up by the large, old-fashioned red damask rose which gives a feeling of freshness, but it would look equally attractive if these roses were omitted and replaced with background stitchery. A further advantage of this design is the little garland of leaves in the top left hand corner, which in itself could be used as a cushion cover design. This is a very simple design with a limited use of shades, making it particularly suitable for a complete beginner. Alternatively, different designs can be created using the lyre, the small basket containing a selection of flowers, and the auriculas.

Dimensions

Finished embroidery (including background)
145 stitches = 14½in(37cm) in diameter
Extra background stitches may be added to enlarge or alter the shape.

Canvas

10 mesh interlock canvas. Allow an extra 3in(7.5cm) around the size of the finished embroidery including the background, therefore canvas size needed:
width: 14½in(37cm) + 6in(15cm) = 20½in(52cm)
length: 14½in(37cm) + 6in(15cm) = 20½in(52cm)

Other materials

Tapestry needle size 18
Colour co-ordinated cotton backing fabric
Cord if desired
Cushion pad 14½in(37cm) in diameter
Zip

Stitching sequence and making up

See page 58 for details. A round cushion should be made up with a zip in the backing fabric, as a good curved shape is difficult to achieve otherwise.

SHADE DETAILS

3 strands of Paterna Persian
yarn
17 shades used

pink flowers
1 very dark pink 900
2 dark pink 910 (2 skeins)
3 pink 912 (2 skeins)
4 pale pink 915 (2 skeins)

green leaves
1 very dark green 530
2 dark dull green 520 (2 skeins)
3 dark green 662 (2 skeins)
4 green 621 (2 skeins)

violas
1 charcoal 221
2 dark grey 210
3 dark purple 310
4 bright purple 302
5 blue 340
6 light blue 343
7 yellow 772
8 orange 801
9 copper 860

Background
very pale olive green 655 (10 skeins)

Creative adaptations

Select particular features of the charted design that appeal and juggle them on a sheet of paper to decide which balance and combination works best. A suggested design is shown in the chart above. Change the colourway if liked, or limit the design to just two or three colours.

Colour the canvas background. Work all the main shapes in the chosen colourway, adding the background last of all. This could be worked in darning stitch (see page 24). For the background, choose areas of stitched lines. These can be either vertical or diagonal. Using a colour from the main stitching, work these lines, leaving unstitched stripes in between.

Wien, bei A. F. Müller, Kunsthändler am Kohlmarkt.

Parrot cushion

Parrots are featured twice as a design in this book, this one being a little more complex than the Needlecase parrots on page 60, but worked on a larger mesh. It shows the typically bright colours of the parrot plumage, so much loved by the Victorians. Even today we enjoy their colour, shape and somewhat romantic qualities and although they are rarely seen in homes, or even in aviaries, we can preserve and treasure them in our embroideries.

Dimensions
Finished embroidery (including background)
120 stitches wide = 12in(30.5cm)
150 stitches deep = 15in(38cm)

Canvas
10 mesh interlock canvas. Allow an extra 3in(7.5cm) around the size of the finished embroidery including the background, therefore canvas size needed:
width: 12in(30.5cm) + 6in(15cm) = 18in(45.5cm)
length: 15in(38cm) + 6in(15cm) = 21in(53cm)

Other materials
Tapestry needle size 18
Colour co-ordinated backing fabric
Hand-dyed cotton velvet (*see* Making up)
Cushion pad 15in(38cm) square
Cord if desired
Zip if desired

Stitching sequence
See page 58 for details on working the chart.

SHADE DETAILS

3 strands of Paterna Persian
yarn
22 shades used

blue wing
1 navy blue 570
2 blue 541
3 light blue 544

green wing
1 very dark green 660 (2 skeins)
2 medium green 661 (3 skeins)
3 turquoise green 683
4 yellow-green D521

orange body
1 brown-red 920 (2 skeins)
2 dark red 900 (2 skeins)
3 orange 852 (2 skeins)
4 bright orange 811

eye, beak and feet
1 black 220
2 yellow 713 (2 lengths)
3 grey 211 (2 lengths)
4 dark brown 920 (*see* body)
5 dark pink 913
6 light pink 915

branch
1 dark brown 450
2 medium brown 730
3 light brown 700
4 yellow 713 (*see* eye)

cherries
1 dark red 900 (*see* orange body)
2 orange 852 (*see* orange body)
3 salmon pink 846
4 yellow 713 (*see* eye)

green leaves
1 very dark green 660 (*see* green wing)
2 medium green 661 (*see* green wing)
3 light green 692 (2 skeins)
4 yellow-green D521 (*see* green wing)

Background
Choose between: pale turquoise 523 (as pictured) or 524 (9 skeins)

Making up

The finished embroidery is rectangular. To square this off and add an extra dimension, I suggest you use a hand-dyed cotton velvet which has been stripped and pieced together.

The velvet should be dyed using soft tones taken from the colours in the parrot and pieced together in the manner of 'log cabin' patchwork, following

Wien bei Franz Barth.

the sequence in the diagram below. The backing fabric for the cushion could also be worked in the same way. Make into a cushion cover following the instructions on page 58.

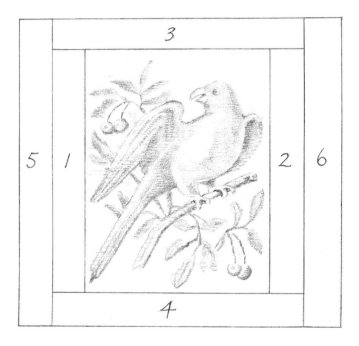

Creative adaptations

An alternative way of adapting this design to a square shape would be to enlarge the needlepoint background.

To do this, take the parrot without any leaves and create a frame of patterned stitchery around a deep, single-coloured background.

The pattern could be created in an area outside the square containing the parrot. Taking the inner square first, stitch the background in tent stitch using a single colour. Border this off with a speckled design using more than one colour mixed in the needle, or by using a random-dyed thread. Stitch the outer border in cross stitch or encroaching gobelin (see page 25) and in a different thread from the single-coloured background. Working this way, you can create a parrot bordered by a single colour to make it stand out, then framed by mixed shades to tie all the colours together, as shown in the chart opposite.

Stitching sequence for the cushions

Work in half cross stitch (see page 23) or tent stitch (see page 22). Outline the size of the finished cushion front onto the canvas and frame the canvas to help prevent any distortion of the finished needlepoint.

Commence stitching in the order of your own preference. Either start from the centre of the design, or work row by row from top or bottom including the background colour.

Block and stretch the canvas if necessary and trim down the surplus fabric to a 1in(2.5cm) allowance.

Making up the cushions

Cut backing fabric to the same size as the front needlepoint.

Placing both fabrics right sides together and raw edges matching, pin and tack together. Using a strong sewing cotton, machine or backstitch these pieces together, as follows. Stitch between the first and second rows of stitches around three sides, and 2in(5cm) into the fourth side at each end. Go over the corner stitches a second time to strengthen them, ensuring the canvas will not unravel when cut away (see diagram).

Remove surplus fabric at the corners by cutting across diagonally, then turn the cushion pieces right side out and place the cushion pad in the opening.

The remaining side can now be slipstitched together allowing the cover to be removed for future cleaning.

Inserting a zip

If using a zip, allow at least 2in(5cm) extra backing fabric. Decide where the zip is to be placed, ie either across the middle or towards the top or bottom.

Cut the backing fabric into two pieces to match the placement of the zip. With right sides together and raw edges matching, stitch the centre seam at least 2in(5cm) in from each end, depending on zip size (see diagram).

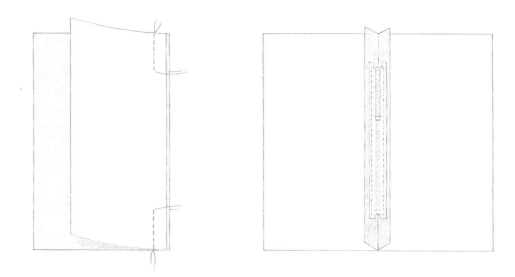

Press open the seam allowance and insert the zip, making equal hems all around. Open one end of the zip slightly to help in turning the cushion right side out later. Place the canvas and the backing fabric right sides together, then pin, tack and stitch all four sides together, stitching between the first and second rows of stitches on each side. Trim excess fabric. Turn right side out and insert the cushion pad.

Finishing touches

To add further decoration, cushions can be edged with a cord (see page 28) which also acts as a camouflage to cover any seams.

A handmade cord using similar colours to those in the design and in a different thread, such as coton perlé, would give a good contrast to the textural qualities inherent in the wool used for most of the stitching.

Needlecase

The bright colours characteristic of parrots' plumage was a natural choice for the Berlin patterns of the Victorians. Parrots also became a popular pet of the period, and were found in most fashionable Victorian homes.

I chose these parrots firstly for their simplicity, allowing novices an opportunity to experience needlepoint without too many stitches and colours, and secondly for the extra benefit of having four parrots to choose from on one pattern. Because this is a small pattern suitable for beginners I thought it appropriate to make a needlecase. On my rounds of different embroidery classes I have found that many embroiderers do not possess this useful item, so here is the opportunity to stitch one for yourself.

Dimensions

Finished embroidery (including background)
170 stitches wide = $10\frac{3}{4}$in(27cm)
65 stitches deep = $4\frac{1}{4}$in(10.5cm)

Canvas

16 mesh interlock canvas. Allow an extra 3in(7.5cm) around the size of the finished embroidery including the background, therefore canvas size needed:
width: $10\frac{3}{4}$in(27cm) + 6in(15cm) = $16\frac{3}{4}$in(cm)
length: $4\frac{1}{4}$in(10.5cm) + 6in(15cm) = $10\frac{1}{4}$in(25cm)

Other materials

Tapestry needle size 22
Colour co-ordinated medium weight cotton lining fabric
Felt for inner leaves
Cord if desired

Stitching sequence

Work in half cross stitch (see page 23) or as in the photograph, where the parrots are in cross stitch and the background in tent stitch (see page 22).

Outline the size of the finished design onto the canvas: this should be the same as the measurements above. Make a choice from the chart, taking either the top or the bottom pair of parrots – with this option the case will be hinged

SHADE DETAILS

1 strand of Paterna Persian yarn
27 shades used

orange parrot
1 very dark brown 420
2 deep red 840
3 rust 841
4 bright orange 822

purple parrot
1 black 220
2 charcoal 221
3 dull purple D117
4 purple 312
5 deep red 840 (*see* orange parrot)
6 rust 841 (*see* orange parrot)
7 bright orange 822 (*see* orange parrot)

eyes
black 220 (*see* purple parrot)
white 260 (1 length)

red parrot
1 dark brown 422
2 dark red 900
3 cherry 902
4 charcoal 221 (*see* purple parrot)
5 dark blue 571
6 blue 340
7 very dark brown 420 (*see* orange parrot)
8 medium brown 432
9 dull gold 750

yellow parrot
1 dull gold 750 (*see* red parrot)
2 orange 801
3 pale orange 710
4 yellow 712
5 very dark brown 420 (*see* orange parrot)
6 deep red 840 (*see* orange parrot)
7 rust 841 (*see* orange parrot)

beaks
1 charcoal 221 (*see* purple parrot)
2 dark grey 210
3 grey D389

green leaf/wing
1 very dark green 660
2 dark green D516
3 green 621

blue-green leaf
1 very dark green 660 (*see* green leaf/wing)
2 dark sea green D500
3 sea green D501

log
1 very dark brown 420 (*see* orange parrot)
2 dark brown 422 (*see* red parrot)
3 medium brown 432 (*see* red parrot)

Background
Choose between: black 220; cream 263 (as pictured); pale blue 344 or 564 (3 skeins)

on the left hand side like a textbook. Note that an extra strip of background at least six stitches wide has been allowed between the two parrots at the centre of the design to accommodate the folding and hinging of the needlecase.

If you wish to alter the combination of the parrots used, ensure that exchanging the parrots gives the same number of charted squares, so that the original dimensions are retained.

For small projects such as this needlecase I suggest working the canvas row by row held loosely in the hand – stitching in the background and pattern all at once. Work an extra two rows of background at top, bottom and sides to be

Wien bei Jos. F. Müller Kunsthändler am Kohlmarkt.

turned over when making up the needlecase.

Starting from the top left hand corner and using the background thread, stitch all the required number of rows needed before any of the parrot colours are reached. Then, using one needle for each shade, start to stitch the design as you work down the chart, keeping the spare needles on the surface of the needlepoint so that they do not get caught up with any of the stitches.

Block and stretch the needlepoint if necessary.

Making up

Measuring both width and height, trim the canvas down to leave a ¾in(2.25cm) border of unstitched canvas for the seam allowance.

Choose a piece of cotton fabric that co-ordinates well with the colours in the needlepoint, and cut to the same size as the trimmed canvas. Mark the centre point of this lining, then put to one side while the canvas is being turned back and stitched down.

Fold under two rows of stitches on all sides. The corners of the needlecase need to be mitred to obtain a neat, even finish (see diagrams).

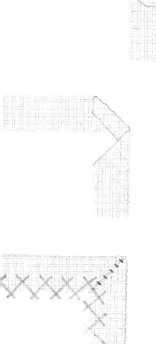

Having mitred and pinned the corners, stitch around the turning to hold it in place. I find the best and easiest stitch to use for this is herringbone stitch.

To back the canvas, make a hem on all four sides of the lining fabric, so that the finished size is ⅛in(4mm) smaller all round than the canvas. This ensures that the lining fabric does not show from the front.

Mitre the corners as for the canvas, and tack in place. Slipstitch the two pieces together with a cotton sewing thread.

Measure the total finished size of the needlecase cover and, allowing ½in(1.5cm) less all round, cut out the felt shapes. Two rectangles will give four leaves, more can be cut if desired. Backstitch in place through the centre fold and all layers of fabric, using a cotton thread. Pinking scissors may be used for the felt to give a decorative edge.

The needlecase is now ready for you to fill with needles and treasure for years to come.

Creative adaptations

One easy way of adapting this design would be to take the parrots without the tree branches and make a repeated pattern with them, even overlapping them slightly to give a busy, colourful design, as shown in the illustration. Then instead of making this into a needlecase, use it for any one of the other projects in this book, for example a cushion or stool top. Use the mesh chart on page 125 to find a suitable size of canvas.

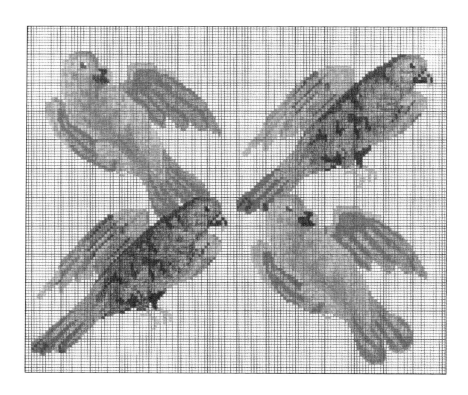

Tablemat

This lovely oval-shaped garland was chosen for its simplistic beauty. The most appealing aspect of its design for me is the grouping of the primulas using differing hues of reds and blues. The beauty of these mats is that you can always make extra ones. I often need additional settings and find that the designs on commercial mats disappear from the market as quickly as they arrive. Although the garland is an oval shape the mat itself is oblong, so it will accommodate any size or shape of plate.

Dimensions

Finished embroidery (including background)

164 stitches wide = 12¾in(32cm)

130 stitches deep = 10in(25.5cm)

Extra background stitches may be added if a larger mat is required

Canvas

13 mesh interlock canvas. Allow an extra 3in(7.5cm) around the size of the finished embroidery including the background, therefore canvas size needed:

width: 12¾in(32cm) + 6in(15cm) = 18¾in(47cm)

length: 10in(25.5cm) + 6in(15cm) = 16in(40.5cm)

Other materials

Tapestry needle size 20

Colour co-ordinated cotton backing fabric

Medium weight iron-on interfacing

Stitching sequence

Work in half cross stitch (see page 23) or tent stitch (see page 22).

Outline the size of the finished design onto the canvas. This should be the same as the measurements above, plus an extra two rows of stiching to allow for turning under when making up. Frame the canvas if you find it easier and commence stitching. Stitch row by row including the background colour, or stitch from the centre outwards, working the background last of all.

When all the stitching is completed, block and stretch the needlepoint if it needs it.

SHADE DETAILS

2 strands of Paterna Persian
yarn
18 shades used

blue flowers
1 dark blue 550
2 blue 551 (2 skeins)
3 medium 553 (2 skeins)
4 light 555
5 pale blue green 523 (2 skeins)

flower centres
1 charcoal 221
2 light orange 723
3 yellow 727

red flowers
1 dark red 900 (2 skeins)
2 red 941 (2 skeins)
3 orange 841 (2 skeins)
4 pale orange 853

leaves
1 very dark green 660 (2 skeins)
2 dark green 610 (2 full skeins)
3 dark sea green 521
4 pale blue green 523 (*see* blue flowers)
5 light green 612 (2 skeins)

brown detail
452

Background
Choose between: palest pink 948 or palest yellow 764 (as pictured)
(4 skeins)

Making up

Trim down the surplus canvas to a ¾in(2cm) seam allowance. Cut the cotton backing fabric to the same size and put aside until needed.

Turning back the seam allowance plus one to two rows of stitching, mitre the corners of the canvas (as described on page 64) and catch down. Tack the remaining seam allowance and herringbone stitch down.

Measure ⅞in(2.25cm) in from the edge of the backing fabric all round and cut a piece of interfacing to this shape. Iron in place on the reverse of the backing fabric. This will give a slightly thicker fabric with a good crisp edge, making it look neater on the finished piece.

Turn under the seam allowance on the backing fabric up to the edge of the interfacing. Mitre the corners and catch in place. Tack round the seam allowance to hold in place.

Position the canvas and the backing fabrics wrong sides together, and slipstitch together.

Wien, bei Ph. Fr. Müller, Kunsthandlung am Kohlmarkt.

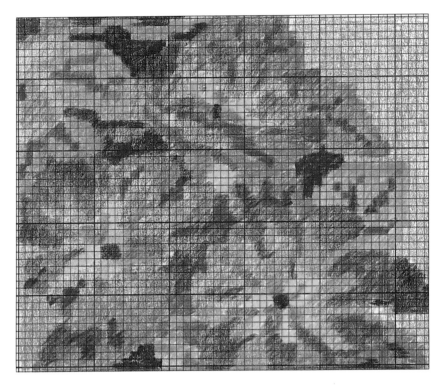

Creative adaptations

Giving the canvas a gentle background wash of colour, alter the size of the flowers into new proportions by taking a section out of the original garland. Take one of the squared areas shown in the illustration for example and enlarge the design to abstract it. Do not worry if the end result is not as accurate as the original chart but, using this as a guide, darn (see page 24) in blocks of colour with a variety of threads and yarns.

For further interest, work the leaves with stitching in the opposite directions to the flower blocks. The length and closeness of one stitch to another can vary greatly; this can help to achieve freedom in the design. Do not worry if bare canvas shows through the stitching. The effects achieved here could be used for a cushion or a framed decorative piece.

Alternatively, you could use a selection of threads in matt, shiny, thick or thin combinations in any desired colourway. The chart could be worked in pattern darning which would produce an embroidery just as hard-wearing as the traditionally stitched canvas and quite economical on threads.

Curtain tiebacks

The function of curtain tiebacks is to hold bulky curtains clear of the window, and they can be made up in a variety of shapes and sizes. Sometimes they are a necessity, but more often today they are simply a decorative feature of the window, alongside the resurgence of the pelmet as a decoration. With this all-over geometric design the patterning is such that the tiebacks can be any size or shape and any combination of colours. The repeating blocks look equally balanced when the pattern is cut into because of the shape produced.
The choice of background colour will depend mainly on the colour of your curtains. You could use either a strong contrast or a subtle blend.

Dimensions

Finished embroidery (including background)

This will vary considerably depending on the size of your curtains. It is advisable to create a pattern, as described in the stitching sequence, and copy this shape directly onto the canvas.

The tieback in the photograph has been worked to the shape given right. The dimensions given are for the stitched area of one tieback. Remember that this area is curved.

291 stitches wide = 29in(74cm)
76 stitches deep = 7¾in(19.5cm)

FOLD

Canvas

10 mesh interlock canvas. Allow an extra 3in(7.5cm) all around the size of the finished embroidery including the background, therefore canvas size needed:
width: 29in(74cm) + 6in(15cm) = 35in(89cm)
length: 7¾in(19.5cm) + 6in(15cm) = 13¾in(34.5cm)

Other materials

Tapestry needle size 18
Colour co-ordinated cotton backing fabric
4 brass curtain rings
Cord if desired

71

SHADE DETAILS

3 strands of Paterna Persian
yarn
13 shades used

oranges
1 dark orange 860 (2 skeins)
2 orange 800 (2 skeins)
3 mustard 702 (2 skeins)

pinks
1 dark pink 902
2 pink D281

greens
1 dark green 661
2 green 663

diamond
1 black 220
2 dark pink 902 (*see* pinks)
3 spice orange 852
4 orange 800 (*see* oranges)
5 dark blue 341
6 light blue 343

detail
white 260

Background
Choose between: royal blue 541 or 542; ice blue 551; mid green 622; pale
pine green 665 (as pictured); pale yellow 704; dark brown 422 or cream
263 (6 skeins)

Stitching sequence

To measure the length required for a particular set of curtains, draw back the curtains, then hold a tape measure round one of them, taking in the fullness and positioning it at the point where the hook should be placed (see diagram). This will be the finished length of the tieback.

Fold a piece of graph paper in half and mark half the length of the tieback on the paper, measuring from the bottom of the fold. Draw the required pattern on the graph paper, then cut it out and try it round the curtains to ensure the shape is effective. The graph paper will help you judge the position of the pattern blocks within the charted design.

Work in half cross stitch (see page 23).

If preferred, frame the canvas. For this design I would suggest you start stitching from the centre fold line outwards. Start at the bottom edge of the canvas so that you begin working the tieback shape at its lowest point, adding and taking away stitches where needed to create a fine curved line. I recommend that the pattern is stitched first and the background filled in afterwards. This will give you scope to make late decisions about how much pattern is stitched.

When the stitching is completed, block and stretch the canvas if required.

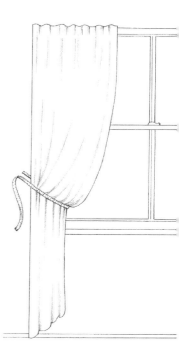

Making up

Trim away the excess canvas to leave a ½in(1.5cm) seam allowance and turn back the hem.

Along the very gentle curve of the sides snip into the seam allowance every 1in(2.5cm) – for the tighter curves at the ends, trim away to a slightly smaller seam allowance and snip into the curve every ¼in(6mm), as shown in the diagram. This helps the curved canvas to lie flat at the edges and prevents unnecessary bulk. Turn back the seam allowance and one row of stitches. Tack the hem and herringbone stitch into place.

Using your template for the finished shape and size of the tieback, mark out the lining fabric and add an extra ¾in(2.25cm) all round for the hem.

Cut out the shape, turn under the hem and tack. Place one of the brass rings on the right side at each end of the lining about ½in(1.5cm) in from the edge and stitch in place. Position the lining on the canvas, wrong sides together, and slipstitch in place. Work a second tieback to match the first.

You may wish to add a cord as an extra decorative feature around the edge (see page 28).

Creative adaptations

Colour the canvas using a toning background colour. Select a section of the design that appeals to you and substitute darning stitches (see page 24) in straight rows for the tent stitch, using a variety of plain and textured threads. Enlarge the design so that it is easier to work. Alter the block of colour according to the progress of the pattern. If the scale and colour appear to be difficult to follow, use them as a guide only. This will result in a very free design as can be seen from the stitched sample.

Tray

This chart is definitely one of my favourites. The tonal qualities which are present in the chart give the acanthus leaves a tremendous three-dimensional quality, so that they appear to be raised from the background like a wood carving. In fact, a wood carver would have a wonderful time using this design as inspiration. Only the circular design has been used for the tray but the extra border could also be stitched, as suggested in the adaptations below.

Dimensions
Finished embroidery (excluding background)
114 stitches wide = 8¼in(21cm)
111 stitches deep = 8in(20cm)
The background has been extended to a 9in(23cm) square in order to fit the tray base.

Canvas
14 mesh interlock canvas. Allow an extra 3in(7.5cm) around the size of the finished embroidery including the background, therefore canvas size needed:
width: 9in(23cm) + 6in(15cm) = 15in(38cm)
length: 9in(23cm) + 6in(15cm) = 15in(38cm)

Other materials
Tapestry needle size 20
Square tray to take embroidery 9in(23cm) square

Wien, bei A. O. F. Müller, Kunsthandlung am Kohlmarkt.

SHADE DETAILS

2 strands of Paterna Persian
yarn
16 shades used

pink centre
1 maroon 901
2 dark pink 905
3 pink 915
4 white 260

yellow petals
1 maroon 901 (*see* pink centre)
2 dull gold 723
3 gold 726
4 pale yellow 715

green leaf
1 charcoal 221 (2 skeins)
2 very dark green 660
3 dark green D516 (2 skeins)
4 medium green D522 (2 skeins)
5 pale green 664

leaf surrounds
1 charcoal 221 (*see* green leaf)
2 maroon 901 (*see* pink centre)

blues
1 charcoal 221 (*see* green leaf)
2 dark blue 500
3 medium blue 502
4 light blue 555

Background
Choose between black 220 or dark red 900 (as pictured) (4 skeins)

Stitching sequence

Work in half cross stitch (see page 23) or tent stitch (see page 22). Outline the finished size of the design onto the canvas. This should be the same as the measurements given above.

Frame the canvas if preferred and commence stitching. I suggest that the stitching is worked from the centre point outwards, working on a particular shape or leaf at any one time. Block and stretch the needlepoint if necessary.

Making up

Trim the canvas to the required size. Unscrew one end of the tray and carefully remove the glass and backing boards. Lace the canvas to the piece of hardboard, then reassemble.

Creative adaptations

With this chart we already have the added benefit of the border pattern, which could be used in conjunction with the main motif on a cushion or possibly on its own as an alternative to the picture ribbon (see page 102), which is based on a straight line. It may also be used as a picture/mirror frame. Refer to the basic techniques section on page 31 for an explanation of how to turn a straight design at right angles for a frame and see the photograph below for a possible design.

Altering the scale of canvas for the working of this chart will give widely diverse results. The main motif, for example, could look entirely different if it was worked on large rug canvas in cross stitch, or on very fine canvas using tent stitch in silk thread with beads added.

Don't forget that any of the colourways could be altered to complement the interior decor of the room in which this design will be displayed.

Firescreen

This firescreen design will not only appeal to the embroiderer but also to the naturalist or anyone with an interest in wildlife. Butterflies are the most easily recognised insect, due largely to their unrivalled variety and brilliance of colour. The complex, kaleidoscopic range of patterns and their delicate beauty are what attract most craftworkers. Butterflies have been used in designs over the centuries and here we have a very fine example of Victorian art. The firescreen provides an excellent way of displaying the needlework.

Dimensions

Finished embroidery (excluding background)
124 stitches wide = 12½in(31.5cm)
168 stitches deep = 17in(43cm)
In order to fit the firescreen surround shown in the photograph the chart has been extended using the background shade, to measure 20¼in(51.5cm) × 14¾in(38cm).

Canvas

10 mesh interlock canvas. Allow an extra 3in(7.5cm) around the size of the finished embroidery including the background, therefore canvas size needed:
width: 14¾in(38cm) + 6in(15cm) = 20¾in(53cm)
length: 20¼in(51.5cm) + 6in(15cm) = 26¼in(66.5cm)

Other materials

Tapestry needle size 18
1 firescreen surround to take an embroidery size 20¼in(51.5cm) × 14¾in(38cm)

Stitching sequence

Work in half cross stitch (see page 23) or tent stitch (see page 22). Outline the size of the finished design onto the canvas. This should be the same as the measurements above. Needlepoint of this size is better framed.

There is a choice between three different ways of stitching this fairly com-

SHADE DETAILS

3 strands of Paterna Persian yarn
33 shades used

brown/orange wing
1 very dark brown 420
2 dark brown 410
3 pale orange 725
4 orange 800
5 very dark orange 720

yellow/orange/blue wing
1 very dark brown 420 (*see* brown/orange wing)
2 red 840
3 rust 852
4 yellow 713 (2 skeins)
5 pale orange 725 (*see* brown/ orange wing)
6 orange 800 (*see* brown/ orange wing)
7 dark royal blue 540
8 dark blue 340
9 medium blue 341

purple/red/brown wing
1 purple D117
2 medium purple 312
3 pale pink 326
4 red 903
5 charcoal 221 (2 skeins)
6 darkest brown 421

striped wing
1 darkest brown 421 (*see* purple/red/brown wing)
2 red 840 (*see* yellow/orange/ blue wing)
3 rust 852 (*see* yellow/orange/ blue wing)
4 charcoal 221 (*see* purple/ red/brown wing)
5 light grey 202 (2 skeins)
6 fawn 465

various bodies
1 very dark grey 210
2 dark grey 211
3 dark steel grey 200 (2 skeins)
4 medium grey 201
5 light grey 202 (*see* striped wing)
6 khaki brown 641
7 blue-green 532

blue wing
1 dark blue 340 (*see* yellow/ orange/blue wing)
2 medium blue 341 (*see* yellow/ orange/blue wing)
3 light blue 342
4 pale blue 344

purple underwing
5 purple D117 (*see* purple/ red/brown wing)
6 pale purple D137
7 charcoal 221 (*see* purple/ red/brown wing)
8 pale orange 725
(*see* brown/orange wing)

large top wing
1 charcoal 221 (*see* purple/ red/brown wing)
2 dark grey 200 (*see* various bodies)
3 light grey 202 (*see* striped wing)
4 pale yellow 654
5 light yellow 727

wing tips (large)
1 dark navy blue 570
2 navy blue 571

eyes
sea green D502

Background
pale butterscotch 704 (15 skeins)

plex design: firstly, stitching from the centre point outwards; secondly, row by row; thirdly, section by section. I recommend you start in one corner initially, stitching row by row, but once the pattern has been established finish each separate butterfly before moving onto another, otherwise you would have too many colours on the go at once. Stitch all butterflies before stitching the back-

Wien, bei P. F. Müller, Kunsthandler am Kohlmarkt.

ground colour. Ignore the half-produced butterflies where the repeating pattern would have started again, filling this area with the background colour. These are only to be used if you are trying to line up and match a repeating block of butterflies. Block and stretch if necessary.

Making up

Remove the back panel together with the hardboard panel from the firescreen surround. Fit the canvaswork to the hardboard panel by lacing with strong twine, vertically and horizontally across the rear of the hardboard panel, as described on page 113. Fit this and the back panel back into the frame.

Secure the firescreen legs by glueing and screwing in place with the screws provided by the manufacturer.

Creative adaptations

The original owner of this chart has obviously had the idea of taking out particular butterflies and making a new design with them, as you can see from the pencil lines on the chart. This would work very well for a smaller project.

The whole design would adapt well to a stool cover or a cushion. For either of these, a substitution of threads would create an interest in the subtle changes of colours that are inherent in the butterflies. Using very shiny rayon threads next to a dull cotton or a soft wool would result in a carved textural quality to the design, as shown in the stitched sample.

Stool cover

The dramatic shape of the diamond alongside the bold use of colours give this stool cover its appeal. A three-dimensional quality is attained by using black as a background – this could be altered to suit a quieter mood by using a paler colour. The quality of this design is based on a repeating motif, which gives us the benefit of having any combination of repeats and therefore any size of stool.

Dimensions

One repeating unit (excluding background)
238 stitches wide = 19½in(50cm)
81 stitches deep = 6¾in(17cm)
For the stool cover, two repeating units are worked (as shown in the chart) plus a further six rows at top and bottom (repeating the acorn design but not the diamonds) to increase the size of the completed embroidery to 14½in(37cm) wide by 19½in(50cm) long.

Canvas

12 mesh interlock canvas. Allow an extra 3in(7.5cm) all around the design including background, therefore canvas size:
width: 19½in(50cm) + 6in(15cm) = 25½in(65cm)
length: 14½in(37cm) + 6in(15cm) = 20½in(52cm)

Other materials

Tapestry needle size 20
Self-upholster stool to take embroidery 19½ × 14½in(50 × 37cm)

Wien bei IC. F. Müller Kunsthändler am Kohlmarkt.

SHADE DETAILS

2 strands of Paterna Persian
yarn
19 shades used

border
1 orange 700 (2 skeins)
2 yellow 712 (2 skeins)
3 red 840 (3 skeins)
4 deep brown (2 skeins)
5 dark grey D346 (2 skeins)
6 charcoal 221 (6 skeins)
7 pale grey D392
8 flesh pink 494

blue diamond
1 dark 540 (2 skeins)
2 medium 341 (1 full skein)
3 pale 344 (2 skeins)

dark green leaf
1 very dark 660 (2 skeins)
2 dark D516 (4 skeins)
3 medium D522 (2 skeins)

mid green leaf
1 very dark 660 (*see* dark green
leaf)
2 dark D516 (*see* dark green leaf)
3 light 692 (3 skeins)

light green leaf
1 very dark 660 (*see* dark green
leaf)
2 dark D516 (*see* dark green leaf)
3 light 692 (*see* mid green leaf)
4 pale 693 (3 skeins)
5 bright 671

acorn
1 dark brown 440
2 medium brown 731
3 yellow 712 (*see* border)

Background
charcoal 221 (*see* border)

Stitching sequence

Work in half cross stitch (see page 23) or tent stitch (see page 22). Outline the size of the finished design onto canvas. This should be the same as the measurements above.

Frame up if required and commence stitching. Note that the design in the red border of one of the diamonds has been painted as a mirror image of the others. The stool cover in the photograph has been stitched so that all four diamonds are the same. This pattern is a suitable one for following row by row. I suggest that you work each diamond block separately so that you do not have too many colours threaded at any one time.

Block and stretch the canvas if necessary.

Making up

Trim the surplus unworked canvas into a rectangle, leaving a 1in(2.5cm) border all round the design. Lay the canvas right side down on a clean, flat surface. Place the stool pad right side down on top, making sure that it is centred on the canvas. Squeeze the pad down onto the canvas, for example by kneeling on it. Bring the canvas over onto the base of the pad and tack it down using ¼in(3mm) tacks, in the centre of each side.

Now tack down each side in turn, working from the centre outwards. The canvas could also be fixed with a staple gun or by being laced with fine twine, as described for the picture (page 113).

If desired, a piece of calico or similar material can be sewn or glued to the underside of the pad before fitting it into the frame. Replace the pad in the frame and rescrew to fit.

Creative adaptations

This pattern could also be used as a rug design. The big, bold shapes and the basic repeat mean that any size of rug could be made. A rug would be worked on an 8 mesh or coarser canvas and should be stitched in cross stitch for stability of the threads and extra durability.

By mixing the stitches used, a subtle textural quality can be achieved. As a further adaptation, the pattern could take on a slightly different shape if the original design were squared off. Place a mirror from one corner across to the other (see page 31) and copy the mirror image.

Even more possibilities can be seen by just observing the chart. The diamond shape on its own could be used as a diamond cushion or could be used as a repeat, omitting the acorn leaves. There are many slight adaptations that can be experimented with. The sketch shows some possibilities. However, care must be taken at all times that the new pattern is transferred correctly onto the canvas to ensure that the outline of the pattern is correct.

Bellpull

The wonderful shape and positioning of these Canterbury bell flowers give this design its main characteristics, and the subtle shading of the colours is carefully balanced to produce a refreshingly natural image. The trumpet flower shape dominates the leaves, yet the design still retains those qualities inherent in most of the plant world – proportion and balance. In the flower language of the Victorians, Canterbury bells meant acknowledgement: an appropriate symbol for this project.
The chart shows how to repeat the design at the top and the bottom, so that any length can be worked. In the bellpull photographed, one and a half repeats have been stitched. The width of the embroidery will depend on the width of your hanging devices. The amount of background yarn specified is for a bellpull 5in(13cm) wide and 24¾in(63cm) long.

Dimensions

For pattern repeat (excluding background)
64 stitches wide = 4½in(11.5cm)
231 stitches long = 16½in(42cm)

An extra twelve stitches have been added to the width to make the completed embroidery 5in(13cm) wide to fit the bellpull ends, plus 10 rows at top and bottom to frame the design and allow for turnovers.

Canvas

14 mesh interlock canvas. Allow an extra 3in(7.5cm) all around the size of the design *including* the background, therefore canvas size needed:
width: 5in(13cm) + 6in(15cm) = 11in(28cm)
length: [16½in(42cm) × 1½] + 6in(15cm) = 30¾in(78cm)

Other materials

Tapestry needle size 20
Bellpull top and bottom (brass)
Colour co-ordinated cotton backing fabric

SHADE DETAILS

2 strands of Paterna Persian
yarn
15 shades used

blue-green leaves
1 medium D501
2 light D502

green leaves
1 very dark 660
2 dark 610 (2 skeins)
3 medium 662 (2 skeins)
4 light 612 (2 skeins)

brown leaves
1 dark 640
2 medium 641

pink flowers
1 very dark 910
2 dark 911 (2 skeins)
3 medium 912 (2 skeins)
4 light 915

detail
1 yellow 712
2 white 260

Background
sunny yellow 772 (5 skeins)

Wien bei K. F. Müller Kunoth

Stitching sequence

Work in half cross stitch (see page 23) or tent stitch (see page 22). Outline the size of the finished design onto the canvas. This should be the same dimensions as above unless you are working to a different width of bellpull ends. Frame up the canvas if required.

Due to the length of the bellpull it is recommended that the stitching is worked row by row. Have several needles threaded up at the same time and leave on the top when not in use.

Remember not to leave excessively long lengths of thread at the back as this creates too much bulk.

Once the stitching is completed, block and stretch if required. It is important that the bellpull hangs straight.

Making up

Trim off surplus canvas to ½in(1.5cm) seam allowance all round. Cut the lining fabric to the same size as the trimmed canvas.

Turn under all hems on the canvas, including one row of stitches, and pin in place, mitre the corners (as shown on page 64) and catch down.

Continue by stitching the allowance down using a herringbone stitch. Turn under the hem allowance plus an extra ¼in(6mm) on the lining fabric. Mitre the corners and tack the hem down. Place embroidery and lining wrong sides together and pin, then slipstitch in position.

Remove all pins and tacking thread. Fold the bellpull over the attachments at top and bottom and slipstitch in position.

Creative adaptations

This design, with its lovely bell-shaped flowers, could equally well be used to make a border. By using the mirror to achieve a corner shape, as described on page 31 (see also photograph), and altering the threads used, a more interesting adaptation can be achieved. The addition of beads would also give a subtle change in quality. Mirror repeating a block into a four way design would also make an interesting cushion pattern. The colour scheme of the Canterbury bells could be altered to suit any interior.

Alternatively, isolate a small section of the chart using a window template as described on page 45. Enlarge it on graph paper or by taking an enlarged colour photocopy to create an abstract design, and work selected areas in a balance of tent stitch, cross stitch and straight gobelin stitch (see page 24).

Footstool cover

Characteristic features of the Berlin patterns are the realism of the flower details and the skilled composition of the design elements. Here the grouping forms a circular shape ideal for fitting to a round footstool base.
This is a design for an experienced needlepoint worker, since the canvas used has a relatively small mesh and the fine detail in the group of flowers is achieved with 38 different shades. There are no large blocks of colour, so frequent reference to the chart is necessary.

Dimensions
Finished embroidery (including background)
147 stitches in diameter = 10½in(27cm)

Canvas
14 mesh interlock canvas. Allow an extra 3in(7.5cm) around the size of the finished embroidery including the background, therefore canvas size needed:
width: 10½in(27cm) + 6in(15cm) = 16½in(42cm)
length: 10½in(27cm) + 6in(15cm) = 16½in(42cm)

Other materials
Tapestry needle size 20
Self-upholster round footstool to take embroidery 10½in(27cm) diameter
Calico if desired

Stitching sequence
Work in tent stitch (see page 22) or half cross stitch (see page 23). Outline the size of the finished design onto the canvas. This should be the same as the measurements above.

Frame up if preferred. Begin stitching in the centre of the design and work the yellow flower completely before moving to an adjacent flower. Work the whole chart before stitching the background.

Once the stitching is completed, block and stretch the canvas if necessary.

SHADE DETAILS

2 strands of Paterna Persian yarn
38 shades used

yellow flower
1 dark gold 731
2 light gold 733
3 yellow 703
4 pale yellow 773
5 palest yellow 764

pink flowers
1 very dark pink 902
2 dark pink 960
3 pink 962
4 pale pink 963

orange flower
1 very dark orange 860
2 dark orange 850
3 orange 820
4 pale orange 801

grey-white flower
1 dark grey 211
2 grey 212
3 silver grey 392
4 pale silver grey 256
5 white 260

blue flowers
1 very dark blue 571
2 bright blue 551
3 mid blue 543

purple flower
1 very dark purple 320
2 dark purple 310
3 purple 312
4 mauve 313
5 pale mauve 314

warm green leaves
1 very dark green 660
2 dark green 610
3 green 611
4 pale green 612
5 pale yellow green 693

cool green leaves
1 very dark green 660
(*see* warm green leaves)
2 dark pine green 661
3 pine green 662
4 pale pine green 663

khaki green leaves
1 dark khaki green 450
2 khaki green 640
3 pale khaki 642

Background
steel grey 201 (7 skeins)

Making up

To make up the footstool, cut the worked canvas into a circle, leaving a 1in(2.5cm) border of unworked canvas all round the design.

Lay the canvas right side down on a flat surface. Place the footstool pad right side down on top making sure that it is centred on the canvas. Squeeze the pad down onto the canvas, for example by kneeling on it.

Bring the canvas over onto the base of the pad and tack it down with a ¼in(3mm) tack. Do the same at a point opposite the first, then repeat at the two remaining points of the compass. Check that the design is still centred.

Next, fold the canvas over onto the back of the pad between two of these points, pleating and tacking the excess as you do so (see diagram). The canvas could also be fixed with a staple gun or by being laced with fine twine.

If desired, a piece of calico or similar material can be sewn or glued to the

Hertz & Wegener in Berlin.

underside of the pad before fitting it into the frame. Replace the pad in the frame and rescrew to fix.

Creative adaptations

A simple change of background colour to cream or pale yellow would make a dramatic difference to the appearance of this embroidery. The design could also be made into a square by extending the area of background. This would look good as the central panel of a cushion, adding a mitred border in a suitable fabric such as cotton velvet.

A third and most interesting method is to create a four-way mirror image of a selected area of the design, as described on page 31. Move the mirrors slowly across the original design – it is great fun to see what exciting effects can be achieved. When you have found the most satisfying area, mark it with two soft pencil lines. Now take a window template and paperclip the 'L' shapes to the chart, so that only the chosen section is visible.

Start at the centre of the canvas, marking it with a water soluble pen. Following the chart and with the aid of the mirrors, stitch all four parts of the design from the centre point. Thread several needles at once, so that you can progress out from the centre with different colours. Each of the symmetrical parts of the design can be worked simultaneously. The chart below shows a possible design created by this method.

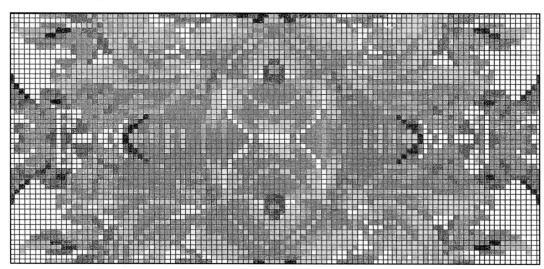

102

Picture ribbon

The appealing design of soft folds of ribbon makes this a popular choice for the traditional Victorian way of displaying photographs, hung on the wall, with a ribbon showing above and below. The strong colours in the original chart will suit any plain wooden frame – light or dark. Victorian sepia photographs would be a good choice to enhance the original colours, or you could try hanging the ribbon between two pictures made up from the designs in this book.

Dimensions

Finished embroidery (including background)

Upper portion   77 stitches wide = 4¼in(11cm)
67 stitches long = 3¾in(9.5cm)
Lower portion   77 stitches wide = 4¼in(11cm)
194 stitches long = 10¾in(27.5cm)

The overall length of the finished embroidery depends on the size of the frame. The ribbon can be made any length by just repeating the folds.

A quicker way of stitching would be to leave the area of canvas behind the frame unstitched, however, this would mean that you could not exchange the frame for one of a different size. The dimensions given above are for the two pieces of ribbon which will show, allowing the frame to overlap the design by ½in(1.5cm) at top and bottom.

Canvas

18 mesh interlock canvas. Allow an extra 3in(7.5cm) around the finished embroidery including the background, therefore canvas size needed:
width: 4¼in(11cm) + 6in(15cm) wide = 10¼in(26cm)
length: 3¾in(9.5cm) + 10¾in(27.5cm) + 6in(15cm) = 20½in(52cm), plus extra for behind frames

Other materials

Tapestry needle size 22
Colour co-ordinated cotton backing fabric
Small brass ring

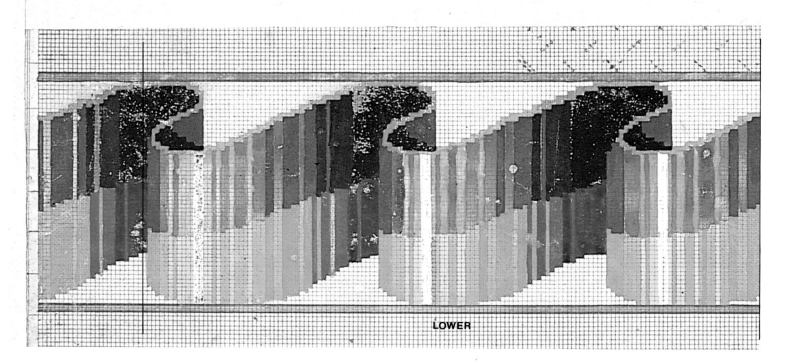

LOWER

Stitching sequence

Work in half cross stitch (see page 23) or tent stitch (see page 22). Outline the size of the finished design onto the canvas, following the measurements given for the upper and lower portions of embroidery.

As mentioned above, if the ribbon is to have the same frame permanently hung from it, then the area behind the frame may be left unstitched. In this case, measure the frame less 1in(2.5cm) and mark on the canvas inbetween the embroidery portions. Stitch the portions as shown in the measurements above and leave the rest of the canvas unstitched.

This design is best worked row by row because of its linear nature. It can quite easily be worked in the hand or, if preferred, on a small rotating frame

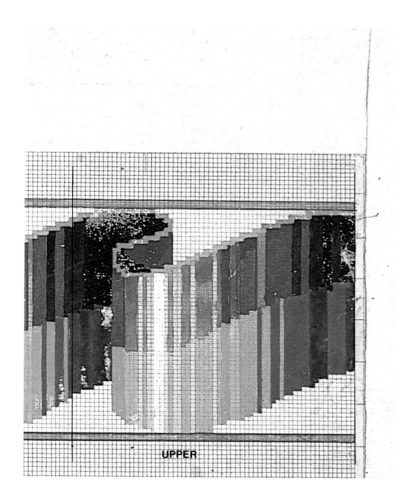

UPPER

SHADE DETAILS

1 strand of Paterna Persian
yarn
15 shades used

border
1 green 613
2 pale blue 506
3 dusky pink 912

brown/oranges
1 brown 422
2 dark red 900
3 orange 831
4 gold 711
5 pale yellow 714
6 white 260

black/purples
1 black 220
2 charcoal 221
3 dull dark purple 210
4 dull purple D117
5 pale purple D127

Background
gold 726

where the excess canvas can be wound round one of the bars.

When the stitching is complete, trim off the surplus fabric back to a ¾in(2cm) seam allowance.

Block and stretch the canvas if necessary.

Making up

Cut the backing fabric to the same size as the canvas. Turn under the seam allowance plus an extra ⅛in(3mm) all round. This prevents any of the backing fabric showing at the front.

Fold back the unstitched seam allowance of the canvas and one row of the stitching, mitre the corners as shown on page 64 and tack the hems in place.

Mitre the corners of the lining and catch in place.

Place canvas and lining with wrong sides together and slipstitch together, keeping the pieces as flat as possible as you work.

At the centre top, sew in a small brass ring from which to hang the ribbon. The embroidered piece is now ready to hang centrally behind the picture. It should go over the picture hook and behind the frame.

Creative adaptations

This is an ideal design to stitch in different colourways, adapted to suit the colour scheme of a particular room. It can be made longer to fit behind two frames hung one above the other.

The original owner of the chart obviously had the idea of working a pattern in the side borders, page 27 gives further examples.

The design looks equally good if a mirror is placed vertically in the centre to give a repeating shape. Move the mirror across the design until you find one that interests you. The photograph below shows a possible choice. This new design could also be used for the bellpull on page 92.

To add greater variety in the stitchery a combination of cotton, silk and wool, stitched in a mixture of cross stitch and half cross stitch with occasional lines of beads added, could give a pleasant textural quality.

Pincushion

This delicately coloured garland with the central butterfly suggests a feeling of peace and tranquillity. The design is worked on a fine mesh canvas in order to fit the wooden base. Working at this scale further enhances the delicate appearance of the design. I personally prefer this design without the butterfly in the centre, but here again you have the choice and either way will look good.
The flowers we see reproduced here – poppies, clematis and tagetes – are typical of the period, and the pleasing contrast of large and small petal shapes helps to balance the design and enhance its delicacy.

Dimensions
Finished embroidery (excluding background)
90 stitches in diameter = 4½in(11.5cm)
Allow an extra three rows of background stitches around the garland pattern for mounting the finished embroidery.

Canvas
20 mesh canvas (10 mesh double (Penelope) will give a 20 mesh if the stitches are worked always over single threads). Allow an extra 3in(7.5cm) around the size of the finished embroidery including the background, therefore canvas size needed:
width: 4¾in(12cm) + 6in(15cm) = 10¾in(27cm)
length: 4¾in(12cm) + 6in(15cm) = 10¾in(27cm)

Other materials
Tapestry needle size 24
Wooden pincushion base 4½in(11.5cm) in diameter

SHADE DETAILS

1 strand of Paterna Persian yarn
22 shades used

butterfly
1 blue 342
2 pale blue 343
3 dark red 900
4 red 902
5 grey D389
6 pale green D522
7 pink D281
8 very dark brown 421
9 brown 730
10 light brown 732

pink flowers
1 dark 902 (*see* butterfly)
2 light D281 (*see* butterfly)

grey flowers
1 dark D346
2 light D398 (*see* butterfly)

purple petals
1 dark D117
2 light D127

Background
black 220

orange flowers
1 very dark orange 950
2 orange 811
3 gold 711
4 yellow 712

green leaves
1 very dark green 660
2 dark green D516
3 pale green D522
(*see* butterfly)

details
white 260
charcoal 221

Stitching sequence

Work in half cross stitch (see page 23) or tent stitch (see page 22).

Outline the size of the finished design onto the canvas, this should be the same as the measurements above.

As the piece of canvas being worked is quite small, you may find it simpler to stitch the garland design in the hand, starting from the centre point outwards, rather than using a frame and working the design row by row.

Stitch the background last, working an extra three stitches all around the garland shape to allow for the making up.

This project should not require blocking and stretching because of its small size.

Making up

The method for mounting the pincushion in its wooden base is basically the same as for the footstool (see page 99), except that finer tacks should be used and pressing down on the pad with your hands is sufficient.

Creative adaptations

This garland will be just as successful without the butterfly in the centre, as mentioned previously. To personalise it, you could also substitute an initial for the butterfly.

Maintaining the same scale, the background could be stitched in fine cotton or silk thread and the flowers stitched completely using small rocaille beads, as shown in the stitched sample. The resulting piece could be used as a trinket box top.

A simple round or square pincushion could be made without the wooden base, if the embroidery is treated as the cushion front and a matching fabric is chosen for the back. Adapt the instructions on making up given with the full-size cushions on page 58, and use a non-flammable toy stuffing to fill the pincushion.

Alternatively, the design could be reproduced on a different mesh of canvas and used as a cushion cover (see page 58) or even as an alternative to the tray design (see page 76), bearing in mind that the tray has a glass cover. Consult the chart on page 125 to find the most suitable mesh size.

Picture

This bouquet of flowers is very typical of the style of design that was prominent in the Victorian times. The forget-me-nots were often seen and are repeated in numerous Berlin charts. I find the colours used within this chart appealing and the blend of greens used for the many different leaves well balanced, whereas they could so easily have dominated it. Once stitched this looks truly exceptional when framed using a simple 2in(5cm) wide wooden frame in veneered maple. This style of frame is very popular now and was often used during the early 1900s.

In the langauge of flowers, according to the Victorians this bouquet of flowers represents love and jealousy. Love is signified by the red royal virgin rose, jealousy by the old-fashioned yellow rose and what appears to be tagetes, true love by the forget-me-not – and the anenome means forsaken.

Dimensions

Finished embroidery (including background)
220 stitches wide = 15¾in(40cm)
206 stitches deep = 14¾in(37.5cm)

Canvas

14 mesh interlock canvas. Allow an extra 3in(7.5cm) around the canvas including the background, therefore canvas size needed:
width: 15¾in(40cm) + 6in(15cm) = 21¾in(55cm)
length: 14¾in(37.5cm) + 6in(15cm) = 20¾in(52.5cm)

Other materials

Tapestry needle size 20
Frame assembly (*see* making up)

Stitching sequence

Work in half cross stitch (see page 23) or tent stitch (see page 22).

This bouquet of flowers is quite complex, therefore it is best to frame the canvas to prevent any distortion. Mark out the dimensions onto the canvas – these should be the same as those shown above. Start stitching in the manner that you prefer: I suggest that this design should be worked from the centre point outwards, completing each petal or leaf one at a time and stitching the background last of all. Add an extra 3 rows of background shade to the top and bottom and 3 stitches at either side, to allow for the rebate of the frame, which otherwise would overlap the design.

If this needlepoint has been on a frame then blocking should not be necessary, but it must be square for framing.

Making up

If you are taking your embroidery to a picture framer, make sure that he or she is familiar with how to treat the canvas.

To mount the needlepoint into a picture frame yourself, the canvas should be stretched over the piece of hardboard that is usually provided with a frame assembly kit.

You may have to trim the hardboard down by ⅛in(3mm) all the way round to allow for the extra bulk of the canvas. To do this, use a sharp blade in a craft knife and score against a steel ruler. Cut the board several times.

Should this prove too difficult, take the board to a local framing shop and they will cut it down for you.

Mounting

To stretch the fabric over the hardboard, you have to lace the sides together using long stitches in a strong thread. Position the hardboard onto the wrong side of the worked canvas. Matching centre points on the fabric and hardboard, fold over the unworked canvas and, using 'T' (macramé) or strong upholstery pins, pin along the edge (see diagram on page 116).

Starting from the centre, securely fasten a long length of strong thread to the canvas and by taking up several threads of canvas with each stitch, work towards the left. After every three stitches hold the lacing thread taut and

Berlin, bei M. Leui Neue Friedrich. Str. N° 54.

SHADE DETAILS

2 strands of Paterna
Persian yarn
39 shades used

purple flower
1 very dark 320
2 dark 310
3 medium 312
4 light 314

blue-green leaf
1 very dark 660
(2 skeins)
2 dark 661
3 mid 662
4 blue-green D501
5 pale blue-green 663

yellow flower
1 dull gold 700
2 gold 711
3 yellow 712
4 pale 714

green leaf
1 very dark 660
(*see* blue-green leaf)
2 dark D516
(2 skeins)
3 medium 612
(3 skeins)
4 light 613
(2 skeins)
5 pale 614

orange flower
1 dark red 950
2 medium red 952
3 light orange 812
4 bright orange 802

pink/grey/white flower
1 very dark pink 901
2 dark pink 904
3 medium pink 905
4 pale pink 906
5 dark grey 202
6 light grey 203
7 cream 261
8 white 260

red flower
1 very dark 900
2 dark 950
(*see* orange flower)
3 medium 952
(*see* orange flower)
4 light medium 954
5 light 945

olive twig
1 dark 650
2 medium 651
3 light 652

blue flower
1 dark 571
2 medium 340
3 light 342

Background
Choose between: pale mustard 715 (as pictured)
or pale yellow 764 (12 skeins)

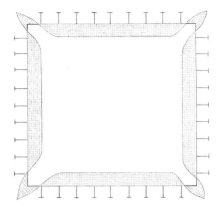 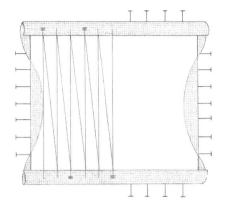 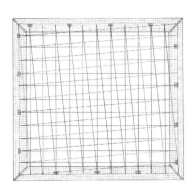

oversew into the canvas several times, as shown in the diagram. This prevents the tension of the stitches from slackening off.

Finish the lacing a short distance in from the edge to allow the corner to be mitred. Return to the centre point and repeat this process to the right hand edge. Once the first two sides have been laced together, repeat the whole of this process on the remaining sides.

Next neaten the corners. They can be mitred as shown on page 64 or you may just tuck in excessive fabric and fold over straight, securing the edge with oversewing. The main criterion for the corners is to avoid unnecessary bulk (see diagram).

Framing

The needlepoint should fit snugly into the frame now without being too loose or causing any bending of the hardboard.

You may wish to complete the mounting process yourself, in which case you will have to decide first whether or not you desire a glass cover on top of the embroidery. This is largely a personal choice, but the protection from dust and dirt could be the deciding factor. Personally, I prefer embroidery to be framed without glass, freeing it from the reflections that glass unavoidably produces. Non-reflective glass is not successful when used with textiles, as it causes distortion due to the textural qualities inherent in the manufacture of the glass.

Should you decide to use glass, then it must be well cleaned before inserting in the frame. Position the glass in the frame. Place the needlepoint face down onto the glass and hold in place using panel pins tacked into the sides of the frame. Care must be taken to ensure that the glass does not crack.

Cover the back of the needlepoint with brown paper, holding it in place with masking tape. Measure one third of the way down the vertical sides of the frame and screw in two eyes, which will hold the hanging cord.

Position the cord so that it does not show above the frame when hung.

Creative adaptations

This chart would readily adapt into a cushion, stool cover or pole screen.

Alternatively, the flowers could be rearranged and repeated in a section of the design, so that there was little green showing through. This would give a very bright, busy design as shown in the chart, with the flowers stitched in different threads.

Tea cosy

This delicate posy of Victorian flowers has a bright, summery feel and using the design on a tea cosy conjures up the idea of a traditional strawberry tea, and the cottage atmosphere this so often evokes.

The design is a very fine one with a large array of colours, which gives the flowers their delicate appearance. Although the yellow irises are somewhat dominant in the design, they are well balanced by the large pale blue hydrangea head and the exotic passion flower. This is a rather detailed chart suitable for an experienced embroiderer.

It makes a large tea cosy or would be equally lovely for some of the other projects as described below.

Dimensions

Finished embroidery (excluding background)

248 stitches wide = 13¾in(35cm)

260 stitches deep = 14½in(37cm)

Note that these are taken at the widest point of the tea cosy shape which is curved.

Canvas

18 mesh interlock canvas. Allow an extra 3in(7.5cm) around the size of the finished embroidery *including* the background, therefore canvas size needed:

width: 16½in(42cm) + 6in(15cm) = 22½in(57cm)

length: 15¼in(39cm) + 6in(15cm) = 21¼in(54cm)

Other materials

Tapestry needle size 24

Colour co-ordinated backing fabric

Colour co-ordinated lining fabric

Thin polyester wadding

Cord if desired

SHADE DETAILS

1 strand of Paterna Persian yarn
36 shades used

passion flower
1 very dark brown 421
2 dark purple 320
3 purple 321
4 grey 201
5 white 260
6 dull blue 341
7 mid blue 342
8 pale blue 344
9 dark rose 920
10 dark red 902
11 rose 903

small blue flowers
1 navy 571
2 dull blue 341 (*see* passion flower)
3 mid blue 342 (*see* passion flower)
4 pale blue 344 (*see* passion flower)
5 white 260 (*see* passion flower)

dark purple flower
1 navy blue 570
2 dull purple D117
3 pale purple D127
4 mauve 333

pink rose
1 very dark red 900
2 dark red 902 (*see* passion flower)
3 dark pink 904
4 pink 906
5 pale pink 947

brown leaves
1 very dark brown 421 (*see* passion flower)
2 dark khaki 640
3 light khaki 643
4 yellow 772 (*see* green leaves)

green leaves
1 very dark green 660
2 dark green 610
3 dull green 662
4 dark sea green D501
5 moss green 692
6 sea green D502
7 yellow 772

yellow iris
1 dull gold 730
2 orange 700
3 gold 711
4 yellow 772 (*see* green leaves)
5 pale yellow 716

orange flower
1 dark red 902 (*see* passion flower)
2 dark orange 841
3 orange 832
4 yellow 772 (*see* green leaves)

Background
Choose between: black 220; very pale turquoise 595; cream 263; very pale blue 546 or pale yellow 764 (as pictured) (16 skeins)

Stitching sequence

Work in tent stitch (see page 22), which will give extra padding to insulate the teapot. Outline the size of the finished design onto the canvas. This should be the same as the dimensions above and following the curved line shown on the chart.

Frame the canvas if desired. Commence stitching from the centre point outwards. This design is quite complex in that the scale is very fine and the colours change quite frequently. I would suggest that, once a line has been established in the centre of the canvas, you work a small block of a particular flower, so that there are not too many colours on the go at once.

If the embroidery has been framed, it should not be necessary to block and stretch the canvas.

Making up

Trim the surplus canvas away leaving a seam allowance of ¾in(2cm). Cut the backing fabric to the same size as the canvas and with right sides together and raw edges matching, stitch together with machine or back stitch, leaving the bottom edge open. Place the stitches between the first and second wool stitches on the canvas. Trim the seams and snip a short way into the seam allowance to ease the bulk of the curved seams.

Using these as a pattern again, cut out two pieces of lining fabric to the same size. Place the two pieces right sides together and stitch as before, again leaving the lower edge open. Trim and snip the seams.

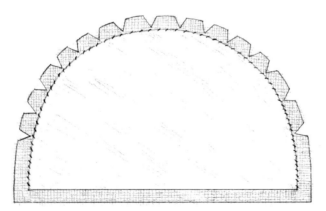

The cosy may be lined with wadding to give extra insulation. Cut two pieces of wadding to the same size as the canvas *less* any seam allowance. Position one piece of wadding on the wrong side of the canvas and catch in place with small stitches into the seam allowance (see diagram). Repeat over the wrong side of the backing fabric. Turn the canvas cosy right side out and insert the lining fabric. Turn under both hems and slipstitch together. A decorative cord may be added to the edge and a tag or a pom-pom may also be added to the top.

Creative adaptations

This design with its delightful posy of flowers would make a lovely framed picture or even a cushion. With both of these little alteration would be necessary; however, if you wanted to use it on a double stool or a long double cushion it is possible to alter the design to suit. My favourite method is to use a single mirror, as described on page 31. With this you can play around until you find a repeat design that is most pleasing to you. Mark the chart with a pencil line where you have ultimately decided, so that it is easy to return to the same spot. This also gives you the line where the mirror repeat will begin.

A more creative choice would be to select a small area on the chart – with its small flowers the hydrangea head makes a very natural choice. This could be adapted using the following method.

Paint the background of a piece of canvas with the colours which are predominant within the design. Apply small scraps of sheer fabrics such as shots, nylon twinkle, chiffons or nets. Hold these down in place by stitching with fine threads in the colours dictated by the chart. Use cross stitch in blocks and add French knots. Do not necessarily stitch all areas of the canvas. The beauty of this way of working is that it allows greater freedom in stitching methods and the additional choice of luxurious fabrics, see the stitched sample for an illustration of this idea.

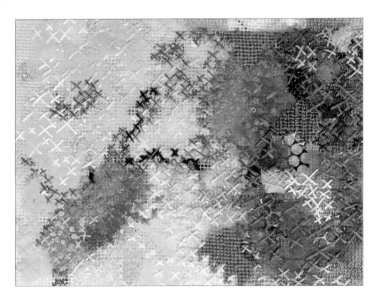

Mesh chart

mesh		8 in	8 cm	10 in	10 cm	12 in	12 cm	13 in	13 cm	14 in	14 cm	16 in	16 cm	18 in	18 cm	20 in	20 cm
spectacles case	45	6.0	14.5	4.5	11.5	4.0	10.0	3.5	9.0	3.5	8.5	3.0	7.5	2.5	6.5	2.5	6.0
	81	10.5	26.0	8.5	21.0	7.0	17.5	6.5	16.0	6.0	15.0	5.5	13.0	4.5	11.5	4.5	10.5
flower cushion	160	20.0	51.0	16.0	41.0	13.5	34.0	12.5	31.5	11.5	29.5	10.0	25.5	9.0	23.0	8.0	20.5
	160	20.0	51.0	16.0	41.0	13.5	34.0	12.5	31.5	11.5	29.5	10.0	25.5	9.0	23.0	8.0	20.5
lily cushion	130	16.5	41.5	13.0	33.5	11.0	28.0	10.0	25.5	9.5	24.0	8.5	21.0	7.5	18.5	6.5	17.0
	130	16.5	41.5	13.0	33.5	11.0	28.0	10.0	25.5	9.5	24.0	8.5	21.0	7.5	18.5	6.5	17.0
round cushion	145	18.5	46.5	14.5	37.0	12.5	31.0	11.5	28.5	10.5	26.5	9.5	23.5	8.5	20.5	7.5	18.5
parrot cushion	120	15.0	38.5	12.0	30.5	10.0	25.5	9.5	23.5	9.0	22.0	7.5	19.5	7.0	17.0	6.0	15.5
	150	19.0	48.0	15.0	38.5	12.5	32.0	12.0	29.5	11.0	27.5	9.5	24.0	8.5	21.5	7.5	19.5
needlecase	170	21.5	54.0	17.0	43.5	14.5	36.0	13.5	33.5	12.5	31.0	11.0	27.0	9.5	24.0	8.5	22.0
	65	8.5	21.0	6.5	17.0	5.5	14.0	5.0	13.0	5.0	12.0	4.5	10.5	4.0	9.5	3.5	8.5
tablemat	164	20.5	52.5	16.5	42.0	14.0	35.0	13.0	32.5	12.0	30.0	10.5	26.5	9.5	23.5	8.5	21.0
	130	16.5	41.5	13.0	33.5	11.0	28.0	10.0	25.5	9.5	24.0	8.5	21.0	7.5	18.5	6.5	17.0
curtain tieback	291	36.5	92.5	29.5	74.0	24.5	62.0	22.5	57.0	21.0	57.0	18.5	46.5	16.5	41.5	15.0	37.0
	76	9.5	24.5	8.0	19.5	6.5	16.5	6.0	15.0	5.5	15.0	5.0	12.5	4.5	11.0	4.0	10.0
tray	114	14.5	36.5	11.5	29.0	9.5	24.5	9.0	22.5	8.5	21.0	7.5	18.5	6.5	16.5	6.0	14.5
	111	14.0	35.5	11.5	28.5	9.5	23.5	9.0	22.0	8.0	20.5	7.0	18.0	6.5	16.0	6.0	14.5
firescreen	124	15.5	39.5	12.5	31.5	10.5	26.5	10.0	24.5	9.0	22.5	8.0	20.0	7.0	17.5	6.5	16.0
	168	21.0	53.5	17.0	43.0	14.0	36.0	13.0	33.0	12.0	30.5	10.5	24.0	9.5	24.0	8.5	21.5
stool cover	238	30.0	76.0	24.0	60.5	20.0	50.5	18.5	46.5	17.0	43.5	15.0	38.0	13.5	34.0	12.0	30.5
	81	10.5	26.0	8.5	21.0	7.0	17.5	6.5	16.0	6.0	15.0	5.5	13.0	4.5	11.5	4.5	10.5
bellpull	64	8.0	20.5	6.5	16.5	5.5	14.0	5.0	12.5	5.0	12.0	4.0	10.5	4.0	9.5	3.5	8.5
	231	29.0	73.5	23.5	59.0	19.5	49.0	18.0	45.5	16.5	42.0	14.5	37.0	13.0	33.0	12.0	29.5
footstool cover	147	18.5	47.0	15.0	37.5	12.5	31.5	11.5	29.0	10.5	27.0	9.5	23.5	8.5	21.0	7.5	19.0
picture ribbon	77	10.0	24.5	8.0	20.0	6.5	16.5	6.0	15.5	5.5	14.0	5.0	12.5	4.5	11.0	4.0	10.0
	67	8.5	21.5	7.0	17.5	6.0	14.5	5.5	13.5	5.0	12.5	4.5	11.0	4.0	9.5	3.5	9.0
	194	24.5	62.0	19.5	49.5	16.5	41.5	15.0	38.0	14.0	35.5	12.5	31.0	11.0	27.5	10.0	25.0
pincushion	90	11.5	29.0	9.0	23.0	7.5	19.5	7.0	18.0	6.5	16.5	6.0	14.5	5.0	13.0	4.5	11.5
picture	220	27.5	70.0	22.0	56.0	18.5	47.0	17.0	43.0	16.0	40.0	14.0	35.0	12.5	31.5	11.0	28.0
	206	26.0	65.5	21.0	52.5	17.5	44.0	16.0	40.5	15.0	37.5	13.0	33.0	11.5	29.5	10.5	26.5
tea cosy	248	31.0	79.0	25.0	63.0	21.0	52.5	19.5	48.5	18.0	45.0	15.5	39.5	14.0	35.0	12.5	31.5
	260	32.5	83.0	26.0	66.5	22.0	55.5	20.0	51.0	19.0	48.0	16.5	41.5	14.5	37.0	13.0	33.5

NOTES: These figures are rounded up to the nearest 0.5 in (0.5 cm). The number of squares for the width of each chart is given first, followed by the depth. Refer to the project instructions to check whether these include or exclude the background area.

Shade conversion table

PATERNA	ANCHOR	APPLETONS	DMC	PATERNA	ANCHOR	APPLETONS	DMC
D117	8550	–	–	420	9666	588	7535/7538
D127	8548	–	–	421	9648	583/584/585/586/587	7515/7533
D137	8544	–	–				
D147	8582	883	–	422	9644	582	–
D281	8364	753	7202	432	9428	184/914	–
D346	9796	–	7337	440	9410	–	7496/7499
D389	9790	153	–	450	9664	338/916	7417/7419/7490/7526/7529
D391	8892	–	–				
D392	8704	–	–	452	9372	955/956	7415
D500	8974	–	–	465	9502	988	7170/7450/7500
D501	8968	525/526	–	490	8254	221/708	7122
D502	8966	524/527	7912	491	9612	707	
D516	9024	–	7408/7540/7541/7956	493	8296	704/705	7171/7179/7460
D521	9288	313/314	7676	494	8292	701/702/703	
D522	9004	831	7406/7452	500	8794	568/747	7336/7590
				501	8792	528/566/567	7297/7306/7311/7591
200	9794	965/966/967	7275/7622	502	8790	–	–
201	9792	964	7620	506	8712	–	–
202	9776	963	7282/7285	520	8924	529	7327/7860
203	9774	151/962	7270/7271/7273 7321/7331/7618	521	8922		7326/7596/7926
				523	8934	522/523/641	7323/7598/7692
210	8720	925	–	524	8874		
211	8718	–	–	525	8912	521	7928
212	8714	–	–	530	8840	159	
220	9800	993	7309/Black/7624	540	8692/8694	465/824/825	7247/7796
221	9798	998	7289/7339/7713/7925	541	8692	823	
256	9782	987	7715	542	8690	464/822	
260	8000	991B	White	543	8688	463/821	–
261	8002	991		544	8672	462	7314
263	8006	882/992	Ecru	545	8686	–	7799
302	8526	452/453	–	546	8682	–	7820
310	8552	606		550	8634	–	7318/7319/7797
312	8592	102/103/104/604	7708/7709	551	8674	–	7317
313	8546	101/885	7241	553	8776	–	
314	8584	884		555	8772	562/563	
320	8530	–	7372	560	8608	745/746	
321	8528	607	7228/7257/7259/7375	561	8606	743	
322	8526	–	7255	564	8602	461/741/886	–
324	8522	602	7251/7262	570	8744	749/852	7299/7308
326	8392	–	7260	571	8636	748	7307/7791/7823
333	8586	–	–	585	8802	–	
340	8610	–	–	590	8922	485	
341	8608	–	–	595	8912	–	7599
342	8606	–	–	601	9080	294/295/356	7396/7427
343	8604	–	–	610	9104	405	7387/7389
344	8602	–	–	611	9102	403/404	7320/7385/7386
410	9642	–	7468	612	9100	402	7384

PATERNA	ANCHOR	APPLETONS	DMC
613	9096	401	–
614	9092	421	7382
621	8970	425/426	7911
622	8984	423/424	7954
624	8982	874	–
640	9314	347/348	7359/7425/7619
641	9312	244/346	7391
642	9310	243/334/344/345	7355
643	9306	332/333/342/343	–
650	9314	245/246	7393
651	9310	255	7364/7377
652	9308	242	7263/7353/7582/7583
654	9302	–	7422/7493/7501
655	8034	–	–
660	9026	297/298/407/647/ 835	7347
661	8992	646/833/834	7348
662	9004	645/832	–
663	8964	–	–
664	9014	–	–
665	9012	–	–
671	9274	–	–
680	8974	429/438	–
683	8988	434	–
692	9156	254/544	7547/7769
693	9196	253/543	7548/7770
694	9212	252	7549/7771
700	8100/8102	–	–
702	8098	–	7474
703	8132	472	–
704	8052	841	7745
710	8122	–	–
711	8098	–	7484/7742/7784
712	8118	–	7434/7726
713	8016	552	7431/7725/7727
714	8014	844	–
715	8012	872	–
716	8012	871	–
720	9540	479	7700
722	8102	476/477	7444/7457/7508/7766
723	8100	475	7767
725	8136	474	–
726	8058	–	–
727	8114	471	7078
730	8064	–	7496/7780
731	8062	–	7781/7833

PATERNA	ANCHOR	APPLETONS	DMC
732	8060	473/695	7473/7505
733	8042	694/843	7504
750	8046	–	7487
764	8012	–	–
772	8116	553	7786
773	8112	551	–
800	9536	–	7922
801	8156	–	–
802	8154	352	7919
811	8166	–	7437
812	8156	557	7740
820	8198	445	–
822	8194	443	–
831	8238	625/865	–
832	8234	442/624/864	7946/7947
840	8204	–	7198
841	8216	446/447/448/502	–
846	8252	–	–
850	8238	866	7303
852	8234	994	7360
853	9534	–	7439
860	8264	–	–
900	8404	147/148/149/227/ 759	7208/7218/7219
901	8404	758/948	7139
902	8402	757/947	7138
903	8418	946	7136/7602/7640
904	8416	944/945	7135/7603
905	8414	–	7204/7605/7804
906	8414	–	7133
910	8424	146/715/716	7212
911	8422	145/714	7210
912	8418	144/713	7205
913	8504	712/754	–
915	8394	–	7211
920	8428	127/128	7115/7199
941	8440	–	–
945	8434	752	–
947	9612	–	–
948	8292	877	–
950	8218	504	7108/7544
952	8212	–	7106
954	8396	–	7103
960	8456	–	7600
962	8454	–	–
963	8452	–	–

NOTE: Where no equivalent is shown, choose the nearest shade.

Index

Acknowledgements

The author and publisher wish to thank the following for their help in the production of the book:

Paterna Yarns, PO Box 1, Ossett, West Yorkshire, WF5 9SA, UK for supplying all the yarns for the projects.

Threadbare, Glenfield Park, Glenfield Road, Nelson, Lancs BB9 8AR, UK for supplying the threads for the adaptations. Threadbare can supply a wide range of embroidery requisites by mail order.

Quail, 21 College Approach, London SE10 9HY, UK for the sleeping cat and the Thai silks.

A G V Harland Ltd, 11–12 Industrial Park, Harbour Road, Rye, East Sussex, TN31 7TS, UK for the stools and firescreen surround.

Lawrence & Lowings Ltd, Lea Valley Trading Estate, Angel Road, Edmonton N18 3HN, UK for the pincushion base.

Framecraft Miniatures Ltd, 148–50 High Street, Aston, Birmingham B6 4US, UK for the tray.

And many thanks to the following embroiderers who stitched the designs:

Audrey Atkin; Sheila Austin; Anne Batty; Judy Brearley; Kathryn Brennand; Christine Ellis; Brenda Farnhill; Eileen Rockcliffe; Elizabeth Shorrock; Dorothy Smith; Glynis Taylor; Dorothy Wilkinson; Marina Williams; June Wise.

Photograph credits:

All the charts: The Rachel Kay-Shuttleworth Collections at Gawthorpe Hall; p8: The Embroiderers' Guild; p9: Robert Estall